THE
COMPARISON
CURE

LUCY SHERIDAN

THE
COMPARISON
CURE

How to be less 'them'
and more you

First published in Great Britain in 2019 by Orion Spring
This paperback edition published in 2020 by Orion Spring
an imprint of The Orion Publishing Group Ltd
Carmelite House, 50 Victoria Embankment
London EC4Y 0DZ

An Hachette UK Company

1 3 5 7 9 10 8 6 4 2

A CIP catalogue record for this book is
available from the British Library.

ISBN (Paperback) 978 1 4091 9122 3
ISBN (eBook) 978 1 4091 9123 0

Printed and bound in Great Britain by Clays Ltd, Elcograf S.p.A.

ORION
SPRING
www.orionbooks.co.uk

CONTENTS

Why you need this book

The contents of these pages apply to you if you have ever looked at someone else, and how they are living their life, and felt a pang of inferiority or doubt that you are enough just as you are. It might be that you've become dependent on social media, and this is causing you to reflect on how you are showing up in your life, or perhaps you do not give a flying duck about the internet but a long-standing rivalry has jeopardised your happiness – comparison does not care as long as it has you trapped.

That's where this book comes in. *The Comparison Cure* is truth serum for your individuality, helping you to make the choices you want. It marks a new era for you, where you will call back your power, end distraction and define and align with the life you want to lead, from today.

As the world's first and only comparison coach, I have made exploring and curing comparison my specialism. I have trialled, tested and, ultimately, perfected a collection of exercises, tools and programmes which have been proved to massively reduce comparison and, in this book, I am putting them in your hands, and encouraging you to heal your comparison wound as I have done.

For more than six years I have helped thousands of people dissolve their comparison complex and reclaim ownership of their thoughts and decisions. I have coached on Skype and in person and taught group workshops. My clients have included pop stars and pub owners, *Harry Potter* actors and hair stylists, school children and retirees.

It is my mission in life to help you get over ranking and obsession with others and instead be truly happy and empowered in your own life so the real you can take back control.

How to use this book

We are about to get started, and before we do, I'd love to share a few pointers to help you move forward with grace and gusto.

Knowledge is power, but knowing how to use knowledge is wisdom.

Throughout the book you will be encouraged to journal your thoughts, goals and feelings, but you will also be delving deeper and learning how to follow through on these – often the missing bit. So, as well as learning about the tricky trap of comparison, this book is packed full of pointers, examples and exercises designed to make you think, and to prompt you to act too.

Each chapter covers a specific step and deliberately builds on the one before it, so for best results, work your way through from start to finish. Make sure you invest the time to complete the exercises as you go, so you can start feeling the comparison trap dissolve straightaway as the real you takes back control. I also advise you to apply the action tips highlighted to your life as soon as you can, and make a note of those that resonate with you the most.

You will notice there is an ebb and flow in the chapters when it comes to exploring themes and concepts, and then the activities and action points that accompany them. With this in mind, treat your reading of this book a bit like interval training at the gym; go at your own pace and with the rhythm of the book. My intention was to be true to my client programme and its process, and this is mirrored in the level of activities included and the weighting of those. For example, Chapter 3, 'Understanding What You Want', is pretty robust – intense even – as its aim is to truly get to the root of your own motivations and is a lynch pin of the comparison curing process. So, although I am not going to apologise for it, I would like to highlight this uneven weighting.

With this in mind, it will also help to approach the experience of curing your comparison like interval training that will see you work different muscles, look at different areas, incorporate different paces to get the result you seek. To continue the physical analogy if I may, this is opposed to approaching it as a gruelling, one-pace marathon.

Finally, I have designed *The Comparison Cure* to be a working tool box for you, so make it your own – scribble in the margins, take pictures of paragraphs that speak to you, fold the corner of pages, highlight the chunks that resonate and repeat and revisit the bits that work for you, to keep your fire stoked. If you need an accountability buddy, I am here – simply tag or add me on Instagram @lucysheridan and prepare to feel my hand on your shoulder!

THE FUNCTION
OF COMPARISON

'Comparison is the Thief of Joy'
Theodore Roosevelt

What is comparison?

According to the dictionary, comparison is 'a consideration or estimate of the similarities or dissimilarities between two things or people.'[1] That sounds fairly innocuous, doesn't it?

Where we start running into trouble is when this practice of the above, and the meaning we attach to it, becomes a habit that adversely affects our life. On the lesser end of the scale, it might be a bit like biting your nails: it's not ruining anything, but it doesn't do you any favours. So, this might translate to an occasional worry about your career and the odd 'bitchy leak' when you hear about Becky from the office flying first-class.

On the higher, more acute end of the scale, a complex can embed itself. This manifests where, from our comparison judgements, we develop beliefs about ourselves and others that lead to mindsets and behaviours that then govern our lives. In life, it feels like being caught in a fog – unable to get out, with your view overwhelmingly affected.

Whether you get the odd pang of jealousy every so often and it makes you feel slightly awkward, or you can identify that your comparison complex is hindering you in your life acutely and regularly, this book will help you.

Where has it come from?

The comparison epidemic we are in now is not a millennial problem but rather a problem spanning millennia. So dangerous was the thought perceived to be, of wanting what others have, that the subject of comparison made it into the Bible with its inclusion in the ten commandments under 'thou shalt not covet.'

> 'You shall not covet your neighbour's house. You shall not
> covet your neighbour's wife, or his male or female servant,
> his ox or donkey, or anything that belongs to your neighbour'
> – Exodus 20:17

It is fair to say that not all the examples have translated with time – I'm okay for a donkey, to be honest – and yet, from this we can judge that our habit of looking over the fences of our neighbours has been occurring since year dot.

Scottish philosopher David Hume was one of the earliest to tackle the topic of comparison and its effects in *A Treatise of Human Nature* (1738–40), his study of malice and envy.[2] He wrote:

> 'A man who compares himself to his inferior, receives a
> pleasure from the comparison. And when the inferiority
> decreases by the elevation of the inferior, what should
> have been a decrease of pleasure, becomes a real pain,
> by a new comparison with its preceding condition'

Ultimately, Hume argued that what grinds our gears is comparing ourselves to the achievements of the people whom we label as our equals. Comparison is most, to use his words, 'painful' when those we judge to be on the same level as us, perhaps due to social circles, age or background, are seen by us to be pulling away.

Comparison and social-status anxiety have been proved to be endemic in more recent centuries too. After all, 'Keeping up with the Joneses' made its way into our collective parlance in the mid-1800s and subsequently evolved into a comic strip that was popular well into the 1950s. Through this idea of 'keeping up' that has passed the test of time, we assess if we are getting along in life by maintaining a status, owning the same stuff and doing the same things as those hypothetical Joneses.

Comparison has therefore been rife throughout the centuries. But why? *Why* do we do it to ourselves?

We owe the official proposal of Social Comparison Theory to the Psychologist Leon Festinger[3], who in 1954 suggested that, as people, we have an inherent, natural drive to evaluate ourselves, often by looking at contrasts between ourselves and other people. As part of this evaluation, we examine ourselves and make various judgments and, from there, we interpret and evaluate ourselves in relation to others.

Festinger believed that we use our comparison tendency as a means to establish a rank or benchmark that we can use to make more accurate conclusions about ourselves. For example, imagine I work in a sales-focused job. I might compare myself to a colleague who has a strong sales record and seems to be achieving their targets every month without fail. If I find my own abilities do not match up, this might motivate me to invest more and improve my own performance in that workplace . . . or not.

Ultimately, the theory looks to the extent we come to know ourselves by evaluating our own results, abilities, views and beliefs in comparison with others. According to Festinger there are different types:

Upward social comparison is when we compare ourselves with those who we perceive to be excelling and advancing more than we are. It's often rooted in our own want to improve our own current abilities or life situation. Because of this, we might look at someone we believe to be doing better than we are and seek strategies to up our own game and accomplish results like they have.

Downward social comparison is when we compare ourselves to others who are perhaps not doing as well as we are. These comparisons give us a bit of a boost and serve to make ourselves feel better about our own situation, potential or what might be going on in our own lives. So, things may not be perfect for us, but at least it's not as bad as another person's situation or performance.[4]

The origins of comparison: it has evolved with us

Ultimately, comparison has always served a function. It helps us explore and understand status in our chosen groups and demonstrates the persistence of our primal human traits to better ourselves, for survival reasons.

Our ancient ancestors lived in life-threatening conditions daily. They organised themselves in collectives of often marauding groups, and it is to this that they owed their survival. To be alone in the world at that time was to be exposed and perhaps end up as a sabre-toothed tiger's dinner if you did not perish due to the elements.

So, using our practice of comparison, we were able to fit in, find our place in the group, be accepted and appreciated by other members.

I can just imagine what would have happened in an ice age:

'Carol those cave drawings have really come along – have you been practising?' (Note to self – I really need to do more to make my cave as attractive as Carol's.)

'I hope this epic fire is warm enough for you, chief – it was my pleasure to collect the wood for you today.' (Note to self – I need to keep my fire-making skills honed so I can keep that job.)

'I'd be happy to join you when we go hunting tomorrow – no, no! No trouble at all!" (Note to self – I need to brush up on my own spear skills or I won't be so lucky next time I come in contact with a sabre-toothed tiger.)

You did and said what you needed in order to stay in the good graces of other tribe members. Using our powers of compare and contrast we could assess our place, manoeuvre, demonstrate our value, preserve our spot in the tribe and our life.

Comparison helps us navigate our way as our social skills develop and we adapt as we go. Adapt or die, right? Darwinism of the most emotive order! By comparing, we select and inherit variations in our appearance, thoughts and behaviours that increase our individual ability to compete, survive, and reproduce.

Who does comparison affect?

Before we throw ourselves into this programme and process, let's just highlight one caveat: it is true that not every single person on earth will experience comparison and its negative effects. These people do exist and walk among us, approaching life untouched by the self-doubt and complex emotions that come with comparing themselves. For them, life is just one big dreamy mood board evidencing what can be possible.

'Oh, you got engaged? How amazing! I am so pumped to meet the love of my life one day!'

'Did I hear you won all the investment your business needed? Congratulations! I am going to do my own thing to achieve commercial growth.'

'Wow – you were nominated for that award? Fantastic! I am going to up my game with my own art – there are rewards out there for me!'

Ironically, in the past I have found myself envying and comparing myself to these individuals, studying them like rare birds, in awe of the self-ownership they possess. Gratefully, these days I feel a bit closer to their mindset than my previous state of feeling crushed by comparison.

But the majority, and if you are reading this that probably includes you, are in my camp. For us, not comparing does not come easily. For us, it will take effort, work and awareness to achieve a sense of ease and occupy that same self-ownership. But we will get there through developing our own understanding, becoming familiar with our own habits and patterns that have led us to spin out in a spiral of comparison.

Comparison affects most of us because it begins when we're young. If you cast your mind back to your own childhood, you can chart its influence. From a very early age, we receive overt feedback and very clear signs that, far from it being desirable for us to just be ourselves, that it's actually unsafe to do so.

- *'I wouldn't be seen dead in that,'* you might have heard a friend say about someone else's party-clothes choices. Note to self: be wary of style choices and follow the majority.

- *'Nobody likes a Debbie Downer!'* a cousin might have teased you, when you were expressing how you were feeling. Note to self: my true feelings could cause other people not to like me, resulting in having no friends.

- *'What? You fancy THAT person? Really?!'* a playground gang may have giggled in your face. Note to self: the person I like must match the standards of my peers, rather than my own.

Let's start as we mean to go on – be truthful and
honest with yourself. Don't be afraid to notice how
this might apply to you in your life. Here, recall
and recollect what memories you have of signs and
indications it was not OK to be you:

Think back to your school years and the law of the jungle that applied in the playground. Who wanted to be labelled 'weird', 'uncool' or 'a loser' during those formative years? Fitting in and going with the crowd meant acceptance, community and safety. The price to pay for standing out from the crowd was at best social awkwardness and at worst falling victim to bullying with its lasting, painful effects. And somewhere along the line, it starts to go wrong.

From an early age, we swap 'what's best for me?' for 'what will be tolerated in the group?' Many of us are plagued by an irrational and unproductive obsession with what other people think of us, which is cripplingly toxic to our individuality, our wants, needs and desires. This can lead to compromise of some kind, whether that's going to the restaurant you don't like that much because your friend likes it, or staying in jobs or friendships that you no longer enjoy. Even the most confident person can be left wondering who they are and what it is they really want.

Perhaps you have invested years of your life in training for a career that your parents made clear they approved of. You could have stayed in relationships longer than was right for fear of being single and what people might say to you at parties. You could find yourself on holidays in places you never actually wanted to visit but the Instagram hashtag pull was too mighty, and you want certain people to think you're a jetsetter. Maybe you live somewhere because you think it's where you should be right now, but the view from the window crushes your soul.

Do any of these scenarios resonate with you?

....

....

....

....

How has your need to be liked influenced you
recently?

....

....

....

....

My personal story

I remember being severely affected by comparison from a young age, so if your memories go back to those early years too, you are not alone.

As a five-year-old I know I looked at my newly born brother and wondered if I was as cute as he was. Then in my school years I made spelling tests and swimming badges a source of comparison, and the ranking continued through my adolescence and into adulthood, where I continued to pit myself against other people in an imaginary game of 'who is winning?', looking to others for markers and validation that I was doing OK.

My comparison crescendo came in my late twenties after I attended a reunion. The day itself was fun and the prosecco flowed with the conversation as we fondly swapped stories well into the night. It felt like the elixir of nostalgia took hold as we recounted younger years and I was able to forget what was going on in my life as, for me, things were far from perfect or worthy of comment. My boyfriend's (now husband's) business had been hit hard by the recession and as a consequence I felt like I was watching a car crash in slow motion as the worst thing we feared would happen became our reality. We were losing our house from under us and I was holding myself together by a thin thread, despite smiling and laughing along with the party atmosphere of the reunion.

As I stood surrounded by people who seemed to have it all sorted in their lives, we added each other on social media. Accepting those friend requests tripled my social networks overnight.

In my vulnerable state this was like fuel to my fire. With more people on my friends list, my sources of comparison and consumption habits went into overdrive, and I scrolled into a hole so deep and dark I completely forgot who I was, where I was going and what I wanted in my own life. From there, the only place was down, and my own comparing habits took an obsessive turn . . .

I would see a 'Fitspo' picture on Instagram and stand for an hour in front of the mirror comparing every line and limb of my own body. I lasered in on three people whose social feeds I would check regularly to keep tabs on how they were progressing. I saved and stored information about people, sometimes taking screenshots of their feeds so I could remind myself what they were achieving. If my curiosity was really piqued, I would go out of my way to stimulate conversations with people just so I could get more dirt on a certain person or scenario I had read about online. My comparison complex made it my business to know other people's business, and yet, do absolutely nothing about it.

It was on a Saturday afternoon two years later that things changed. I remember I had scrolled back through three years of someone's Facebook photos and rolled my eyes at him posting he was visiting the Maldives (again!) when my phone overheated in my hand and the screen went dead. Comparison had literally become too hot for me to handle. How had I ended up there – feeling so inferior, so lost, so inadequate and so unsure of myself, compared to my peers? To everyone, if I'm honest.

And then it dawned on me, if I could think and feel myself into this, could I think and feel myself out of it and reconnect with myself? I had to at least try.

Initially this personal assignment took me to easy-to-access resources like TED Talks and the bookshop's self-help aisle, then I signed up for online classes and subscribed to psychology blogs to gain a deeper view. This then led to more formal training. The more I understood about myself and what motivated me – what I feared and where I wanted to be without anyone's influence – the more I noticed comparison loosen its grip and I earned back my joy. From here, I became truly motivated to pass on what I had picked up along the way.

Is comparison getting worse?

Comparison has helped people through the ages know the games to play and the markers to meet to be accepted and then to excel. As we have advanced as a species, so too has our primal comparison habit and with it the premium placed on rank, position or prominence in our immediate communities and the wider world. And now the digital age means we are waking up every day to a Las Vegas of comparison accessed via our devices: open all hours, dazzling bright lights, anyone welcome and always something new to consume to bet against yourself on the poker tables of your seemingly small potential. For the majority of us, our lived reality feels exactly the opposite and instead of finding inspiration in seeing other people live big, bold, beautiful lives, we can ruthlessly compare ourselves to what they are being, doing and achieving.

The sinister impact of social media on this complex cannot be disregarded:

- A 2014 survey of college students found Facebook use triggers feelings of envy (which were also found to predict depression symptoms). [5]

- A 2018 research paper from the University of Pittsburgh's School of Medicine found that exposure to idealised representations of peers on social media brought on the distorted belief that others lead happier, more successful lives. [6]

- Another 2018 study, by Florida House Experience, a mental health and addiction treatment facility, highlighted that 51 per cent of women between the ages of 18 and 24 said they feel pressure to look perfect on social media. And 60 per cent of women from all age groups said they wouldn't post a photo of themselves on social media unless they loved the way they looked. [7]

The pressure to 'keep up' socially and live a life that looks good has never been so wide-reaching and invasive. With most of us on social media, we are crafting and curating an image of ourselves for our friends and followers.

My view is therefore a clear and pronounced 'yes' that comparison is getting worse. In fact, I would go one step further and say we are in the midst of a comparison epidemic brought about by the power couple that is social media and technology. With it comes a toxic and deep-rooted effect on how we are living our lives, the decisions we are making and how we are connecting with people. All too often what we see online is influencing our abilities to notice and accept how other people are living.

For example, at any point recently:

- Has your finger hovered over the block button because your ex-colleague's career progress is just too much for you to handle?

- Have you avoided seeing your cousin at family parties because their happy relationship status feels overwhelming to be around against your own romantic missteps?

- Have you wanted to give up on your blog because 'what's the point?' when the impact you are making feels so insignificant compared to the influencers you follow?

- Have you found yourself worrying about whether you're on the right path?, 'Am I doing enough to be successful?', 'Can I be loved if I don't do what they do?'

Having a 'personal brand' on platforms such as Instagram is becoming more commonplace, but to say it's solely the approval of others we are chasing is only half the story – our own esteem has a say too as we strive to tickle the tummy of our egos through our posting patterns.

Some of the behaviour I noticed in my own life continues to be a wake-up call for me, for example, I have:

- Let my food go cold at restaurants to capture a picture of my meals and post that I was eating at the newest hot spot.

- Nearly missed flights because I was concentrating on tagging myself on an app rather than listening for my seat row announcement.

- Stalked ex-partners and friends online regularly to check in on their lives and make judgements accordingly.

You're not making it up

All too often it can perhaps feel like we are making something out of nothing – a mountain out of a molehill – when our comparing sends us into a tailspin. This isn't helped when the best advice we are given is 'just don't look!' or 'why does it matter to you what they are doing?' With that comes embarrassment and awkwardness with a side of sheepish thrown in for good measure. I have lost track of the times people have prefaced a statement about their comparison with: 'I know I'm being stupid but . . .' 'This is going to sound silly but . . .' 'I feel like such an idiot to admit it but . . .' 'I am probably just imagining it but . . .'

You are NOT making it up. It's OK to feel your feelings and notice them. You do NOT have to just get over it like it's nothing. Your emotions, experiences, and perspectives are valid. This is a safe space for you to listen to and explore those feelings, and in this book you will be given plenty of tools to ease and, ultimately, dissolve those negative feelings altogether.

Where to begin

So, here we are, faced with a growing, insidious problem that shows no sign of slowing, and yet we are under-resourced and our tools are too blunt to address it. Until now, that is. Choosing not to conform to the definitions of success laid down by society can feel like navigating rocky ground because how we feel has grown to depend so much on what others think of us.

And because there will always be an individual or group that seems to have more of a good thing, how can we possibly be at rest? How can we ever be, do or have enough?

The remedies and solutions lie in:

- Understanding how you can drown out the noise of social media and other people, and on the way, love and accept yourself (be less 'them').

- Achieving radical connection with yourself, your life, your choices and goals and the ways you approach these (be more 'you').

- Taking active responsibility for your own life experiences and your reaction to them so you can live purposefully.

So how can we put these solutions into play and finally overthrow the thief of joy? The confidence killer that sneaks in from the tips of our fingers into the inner workings of our mind. That's where this book comes in. *The Comparison Cure* is intended to tackle these issues head on, so we can stop comparison in its tracks and no longer tumble down the rabbit hole of social media, or become fixated on hearsay we pick up daily about those we might be jealous of.

Instead of succumbing to self-judgement and negative self-talk, we can cure the poisonous tendencies of comparison and prevent its toxic effects from infiltrating our lives. This book will help you move away from comparison, frustration and envy and instead head towards self-focus, increased confidence and finding your inner peace as you learn to live authentically as the sovereign in your own life.

So, here is your formal invitation:

- To understand yourself deeply and to dissolve, let go of and stop doing anything that does not align with you, your values and motivations.

- To find the indescribable freedom that comes with cracking your own code to living #comparisonfree.

- To start spending your time doing things you like, with people you appreciate and in the process reboot your energy so that your cup always feels full.

- To dissolve obligation and replace it with conscious, mindful decision-making in alignment with who you are here to be.

- To peel back the layers of beliefs and programming that have formed in your brain, heart, and gut over time.

- To be a case study of what it is to turn it all around, no matter your life experiences or current circumstance.

Let's get started.

PART ONE

DIAGNOSIS

CHAPTER 1

GETTING INTIMATE WITH YOUR COMPARISON CONDITION

'Remember always that you not only have the right to be an individual, you have an obligation to be one'
Eleanor Roosevelt

We are kicking off at square one, and, just like with any traditional diagnosis, this chapter will see us go into the detail of some of the key functions and symptoms of a comparison complex. We will look at how comparison triggers us, the people and things that trigger us most (including the significance of these) and we will also bring in your own personality traits so you can better understand how comparison might affect you specifically, and the unique abilities you possess to help dissolve your own complex.

'Why on earth would I want to do that?!' I hear this a lot when I introduce the idea of intimacy with our comparison, and it is to be expected. Who wants to hang out with something that makes them feel a bit gross and embarrassed? I get it! But denial doesn't work. Suppressing it doesn't make it go away and rejecting that part of ourselves is to reject our whole self. It is when we build a close relationship with our own comparison habits that we take away their insidious influence in our lives and transmute it into targeted, positive power.

First up, let's look at the approach I take with clients; it is based on increased awareness and understanding about where in life we might be:

- disconnected from ourselves

- distracted by others

- occupied by and focused too much on the actions and goings-on of those around us (whether we know them or not)

- at the mercy of our triggers, activators and comparison personas.

Collectively, these habits and actions encompass a 'comparison episode'.

The Comparison Trigger Indicators and how many resonate with you

There's a good chance that if you are reading this you already have the self-awareness to know what your comparison triggers are, but you might have missed out or glossed over certain ones. As our aim is to become very intimate with our own comparative habits – now is the time to stop and make sure we understand all of them.

Have a read through the following Comparison Trigger Indicators (CTIs) and see which match your own tendencies.

1. You want what another person has, whether it's an outlook on life, material possession or a certain status in the world.

2. On seeing this person, you feel hot emotions in your emotional system and feelings of jealousy start bubbling.

3. You wonder about them; they find a way into your thoughts without invitation and stay there, sometimes for moments, sometimes for longer periods of time.

4. You lose time, consciously and passively, keeping tabs on what they are doing, being or experiencing.

5. You rank yourself against them – they are a measure for how well you feel you are doing in your life.

6. You feel you are in competition with them even though they might be a complete stranger.

7. You dissect and analyse what they say, do and post, looking for holes and inconsistencies because you are 'on to them' and you 'don't buy it'.

8. They stimulate doubt in yourself, your ideas and your own plans.

9. You believe they have more luck, opportunities, resources, time and connections than you do, or you will ever have (most likely based on a handful of facts).

10. You LOVE it when things go wrong for them. Schadenfreude is strong with you when it comes to a particular individual or group of individuals.

This is a good time to highlight the 'Yes to honesty. No to judgement' rule I insist you follow with yourself as we crack the code to your comparison and ultimately aim to cure it for ever. Some of the questions posed and feelings stirred during this reading might be uncomfortable, or even make you cringe a bit. That is OK. That is normal. That is to be expected. I ask that you switch judgement for a neutral sense of observation.

This attitude will allow you to achieve the growth you seek more quickly and smoothly, and will stop you getting stuck or hung up on the judgement. Your aim is to collect awareness points.

* **Action tip:** Instead of thinking, 'Oh God, I do that! Have you been bugging my phone?! This confirms my suspicion that I am indeed an absolute loser!', think more along the lines of 'OK. I recognise that I do that so I will keep this information and use it now or later.' Practise noticing when your Comparison Trigger Indicator hits with a neutral attitude.

* With that said, it's time for our first exercise to help you get on your way to curing your comparison.

How many of these CTIs, highlighted previously, resonate with you? It might be all, or it might be that one of these stands out as a stickler for you. Note down the numbers that match your comparison trigger tendencies here and for an extra credit recall some examples.

Keep this close at hand as we will build on this unique insight – we are off to the races.

Looking at the people you compare yourself to

At this point, I'd like to borrow from the language of the gaming world and introduce you to the idea of the comparison avatar. That is, the figure or person in your life, or in your awareness, that is the subject of your comparison.

If you find it is certain people that stimulate your comparison, you will already know that not all comparison 'avatars' are created equal. You don't have to have a close, working knowledge of an individual's life and accomplishments for them to make you feel less than you are. Comparison avatars can be:

- Resonant/proximate: someone who is in your real world who gets your comparison going.

- Remote: someone you don't know and probably will never know, and yet this person triggers your comparison.

Some of my own comparison avatars are resonant/proximate, in that there are a couple of people from my school days that I compared myself to then, and still do a little bit now. And then every so often a complete stranger will enter my consciousness and they can become an obsession for my comparison if I'm not careful, even though they are entirely remote from my life.

Now, over to you. Remembering that nobody will see this, note down the people or things you compare yourself to:

....

....

....

....

My resonant/proximate comparison people are:

....

....

....

....

My remote comparison people are:

....

....

....

....

However close you feel to the subject of your comparison, the behaviour that comparison leads us to can be categorised into some shared characteristics:

- We withhold love, support, kind words and likes.
  We simply cannot bring ourselves to get behind that
  person and their efforts.

- We are defensive when called out or offered advice. We
  feel touchy when others are not willing to empathise or
  won't tolerate our comparing.

- We experience repeating patterns. We ping-pong between
  begrudging others and bashing ourselves.

- We judge, critique and feedback on the people that
  surround us, whether solicited or not. We can become a bit
  of a know-it-all and cannot resist the temptation to have a
  'bitchy leak' or gossip about our comparison avatar.

These behaviours ultimately cause us pain. It's like going out
swimming in the ocean and smashing a hole in your snorkel and
goggles, then getting annoyed that the water is flooding in and you
can't see.

Rather than setting ourselves up to be protected while we pursue
our goals in life, we let in the deluge. Over and over again we can
find more and better ways to hurt ourselves, our efforts and our most
important relationships.

'Comparison is an act of violence against the self'

– Iyanla Vanzant

But enough now. Enough of the violence and pain that we inflict
on ourselves. It has served us no benefit and brought us no closer to
our purpose.

To turn things around we need to flip the way we look at using
comparison and use it to our advantage to win every time.

Identifying your comparison personality persona

Despite being individuals, we are linked and connected in our human experience and, as such, we share much in common when it comes to comparison. Having helped thousands of people over the years, this is a topic I have been able to study in detail. It has enabled me to spot patterns, similarities, and trends when it comes to personality types and how each type can work with their comparison tendencies, not against them. This next section presents a basic starting point and is inspired by an existing framework that has been helping humans understand themselves, and the world around them, for centuries.

These personas, listed below, are inspired by the Enneagram. I was introduced to this spiritual-development framework when my personal coach at the time, Reverend Gail Love Schock, invited me to take the test and find out my own personality type to help guide our work together. It was one of the greatest gifts I could receive as I have been able to use that insight in my life, especially when it comes to comparison.

Established in ancient times, the Enneagram stems from the Greek words *ennea* (nine) and *grammos* (a symbol). To use plain language, it represents a system of personality types, each governed by how each interacts with, approaches and feels about the world, arising from deeper drivers and motivations. It surfaced in the modern world in 1915, introduced by philosopher and teacher George Gurdjieff. Then in the late 1960s, Oscar Ichazo placed the nine personality types around the Enneagram diagram. To follow this, Claudio Naranjo, MD and other psychologists combined the Enneagram with emerging advancements in modern psychology.[8]

For the purposes of this next bit, I have rephrased and summarised the Enneagram types to provide some first-step insights to help guide your understanding as I found these incredibly helpful when I too was exploring the deeper intellectual work and how it links to comparing. Ultimately it is a necessary reminder that when we see ourselves as alone, solitary or separate, then there is struggle.

Now, crucially, this is not about putting you in a pre-defined box! Oh, the irony if that were the case. This is about how seeing a box can help us acknowledge and step outside of certain perspectives, and through doing so discover conscious and unconscious patterns. This in turn allows us to take more responsibility for our life choices.

To arrive at your accurate Enneagram type you will need to complete the extensive official test, which can be found online and is well worth your time. It is important to note that many people study the Enneagram intensely over an entire lifetime, so the intention here is not to reduce or disrespect this body of work.

Through looking at comparison through the lens of some of the Enneagram's essential principles, however, we can achieve further insight into what might be a barrier to our own self-focus.

So, the next part of your comparison diagnosis is to identify which persona or two might resonate most with you, so that you can become aware of any blind spots that are hiding in the next part of your journey. It will also show you what superpowers, attributes and strengths you have – and you can then use these to combat your own comparison.

The personas: from the descriptors below, choose the ones that you feel you resonate with and relate to most. We each share something in common with all of them, and yet you know in your heart of hearts which are the two that fit you best.

Consider the following statements:

- The friendly one . . . I am easy-going, approachable and I have the ability to see both sides of a story but I can be judged to be indecisive.

- The blunt one . . . I say it like it is and can be relied on to be assertive, but I'm aware I can scare people away with my directness.

- The fun one . . . I hate to feel trapped and love new experiences and have a thirst for adventure, but I struggle to stick to tasks and feel grounded.

- The reliable one . . . I am committed, loyal and hardworking and yet I tire myself out because I worry about things a lot and want to do everything right.

- The analytical one . . . I love to observe, learn and apply my knowledge but I can struggle with social situations and feeling heard in a group.

- The sensitive one . . . I often feel fragile and I can be easily hurt by other people, especially if I feel ignored.

- The striving one . . . I'm goal focused and ambitious, but my obsession with achievement means I rarely stand still or feel satisfied.

- The people-pleasing one . . . I find it hard, if not impossible, to say 'no' and my need to be liked can stop me from being myself.

- The perfectionist one . . . For me, everything has to be just so and sometimes I set expectations that feel impossible.

Give these statements another read through before you make your decision and arrive at one or two personas that fit. There is a good chance that two or more may resonate with you. Make sure to choose the one that feels like it would be the best fit for you and who you are. When you are ready, turn over and digest the guidance . . .

Persona descriptor	It is important to be aware that ...	So, use your superpower, which is ...
The friendly one ... I am easy going, approachable and I have the ability to see both sides of story but I can be judged to be indecisive.	You care a lot about what other people think of you and find it hard not to take things personally. This can cause hesitation and stop you from moving forward and acting on your initiative.	You have a gift for going with the flow and being aware of the here and now – use this awareness to ensure you are taking action for yourself.
The blunt one ... I say it like it is and can be relied on to be assertive, but I'm aware I can scare people away with my directness.	You put too much pressure on yourself to do things in a certain way and it becomes beyond frustrating when things don't work as you are pushing them to.	You are able to take charge and meet challenges head on – galvanise that quality for your own success.
The fun one ... I hate to feel trapped and love new experiences and have a thirst for adventure, but I struggle to stick to tasks and feel grounded.	You run out of time to finish off tasks because you are trying to move onto and fit in the next thing.	You have such varied interests and abilities, have the guts to take risks and to try exciting adventures.
The reliable one ... I am committed, loyal and hardworking and yet I tire myself out because I worry about things a lot and want to do everything right.	By constantly scanning situations for risk and danger you can fall into procrastination and lose time because you find it difficult to make up your mind.	Your intellect, tenacity and ability to shoulder responsibility can be a great source of courage – don't just save these to use for other people – be loyal to yourself too.
The analytical one ... I love to observe, learn and apply my knowledge but I can struggle with social situations and feeling heard in a group.	You delay sharing your own knowledge and gifts and have to witness other people who are less experienced succeed or be perceived to overtake you.	You are gifted at spotting and knowing the facts of a situation and coming to a meaningful understanding of what step comes next, so take it!

Persona descriptor	It is important to be aware that ...	So, use your superpower, which is ...
The sensitive one ... I often feel fragile and I can be easily hurt by other people, especially if I feel ignored.	A belief you have is that you don't deserve to be loved and the fear of disappointing people can keep you feeling stuck and fearful of even trying.	Your ability to feel deeply is an invaluable GPS system to guide you to move forward with your own path. Use it to your advantage.
The striving one ... I'm goal focused and ambitious, but my obsession with achievement means I rarely stand still or feel satisfied.	Being seen as successful is a big motivator that can mean comparison is particularly acute for you as you rank yourself against other people regularly to track your progress.	You make things happen and keep things working efficiently as well as bringing people with you through your inspiring ideas and actions. Harness these valuable skills.
The people-pleasing one ... I find it hard, if not impossible, to say 'no' and my need to be liked can stop me from being myself.	You can be left feeling depleted and frustrated with where you are because you rarely say 'no' to requests and demands made of you.	You are warm, kind and you really, really care about people, which is obvious when you walk into a room. Let yourself channel your enthusiasm, positivity and nurturing nature into yourself.
The perfectionist one ... For me, everything has to be just so and sometimes I set expectations that feel impossible.	Because you are such a hands-on person, you can juggle lots of tasks and shoulder responsibility, which ties up your time and energy, leading to you being distracted by other people's progress.	Nobody can compete with the commitment you can show to something important to you – turn that bottomless self-discipline onto yourself.

From reading the one or two descriptors, how does this land with you? Again, the intention is not to pigeonhole you but to provide some priority pointers so you know the perspective to be aware of when approaching your own cure for your comparison.

I tend to use the awareness point to signpost what traits might get in the way of my comparison-curing efforts and the super power as my rallying cry to use those attributes for myself as I do so freely with others.

....

Action tip: Make a note or take a picture of the descriptors, awareness points and super powers that apply to you, as written here, and put them somewhere prominent so you can see them every day and be inspired to act on this information. For extra credit, seek out the Enneagram test via the Enneagram Institute and search for Gail Love Schock (@gail_loveschock) and take your understanding even deeper – this is a fascinating and revealing area of personal study.

....

Finding the insight in our own comparative behaviours

Our attention will now turn to what is at the root of why we're comparing ourselves to others and what we can do to flip comparison on its head.

When I was a kid there was a TV quiz show called *The Crystal Maze*. The premise was each contender would answer a question correctly in order to have a go at solving the puzzle. Each one would have a certain theme and the aim of the game was to complete the puzzle and, in return, win a crystal. The quiz contender, on getting their hands on that sparkling glass token, was free to move on to the next challenge and win even more points. Ultimately the aim was to get in, get the crystal and get out again. Bish, bash, bosh!

This is how I'd like you to view comparison, its triggers and the avatars that prompt them. The crystal in this analogy is the insight that our comparison avatars present us with – the puzzles within which to find our jewel. The insight will usually be understanding what is going on in your own life that is causing you to feel jealousy or frustration about the other person's situation.

When we get to it, we can take action to power fiercely self-focused efforts. So much so that you will stop giving a hoot about what anyone else is doing, whether you see them every day or they are a stranger on the internet.

How might we further seek our crystal of insight? Let me share some examples to get your puzzle-solving powers buzzing, as we will be applying this magic, works-every-time technique to your life in a moment.

Case study 1: from air miles to more smiles

A client came to see me and from the moment we started talking she reeled off her frustration at seeing a former colleague leading what appeared to be a jet-set lifestyle.

The client, let's call her Jamie, was triggered at seeing this person checking in at airport departure lounges, she was seeing red on reading her posts that showed yet another sunset in another far-off land. All this while Jamie was yo-yo-ing between feeling stuck on her commute and feeling physically attached to her work desk.

I heard her out and let her get her feelings off her chest. It was then that we lasered in to find the information this comparison episode was waiting to reveal. It soon became clear that Jamie had her own passion for adventure and an unanswered wanderlust within her that had been lying frustratingly dormant. Travel was her 'thing', and always had been since she had been old enough to have her own passport. Despite this, it had been four years since she had had any meaningful time away.

It began to dawn on her that her own situation had nothing to do with how many air miles her former colleague was piling up and had everything to do with her own lack of rest and adventure. 'Why did I think I could only live my love of travel in my twenties? I am the only one that has stopped me from getting away!'

With this realisation came her desire to act. Following our session, she walked into her boss's office and sat down to discuss the time she wanted to book off for the year ahead. To her surprise, her boss was relieved and happy she was doing so as they had noticed her sparkle dim and were worried about the hours she was putting in to the cost of her personal life.

Summary:

☐ **The comparison episode was brought on by** being jealous of seeing someone else travelling and experiencing new things.

☐ **The crystal of insight here was** the realisation that Jamie had an unanswered call to travel within her that she had been ignoring for years.

☐ **The next step was to act on the insight** and book off time from work. This allowed her to stay committed and get excited, knowing that her own version of adventure was now secured and promised to her.

☐ **The change that sticks:** I often get tagged on her pictures of sunsets from the trips that she now regularly takes.

☐ Case study 2: from romantic rut to a restored relationship

This next example is related to Jay, who came to work with me to cure his comparison in the area of love and relationships. He had found that he had become obsessed with looking at other couples setting up their own homes, taking trips together, having regular date nights or bringing each other cups of tea. It was making him feel like his relationship had gone stale or ground to a halt. He found himself feeling so jealous as he watched the gestures that other people were making to each other, and the public declarations of love on social media were becoming a bit too much to handle.

Through my questioning, it became clear that as much as Jay was frustrated by the lack of romance coming from his partner, he too had not made any effort recently. He had fully participated in the current stale situ.

Jay realised he could not ask something from his partner that he was not doing himself. He also realised he couldn't expect someone else to know what it was he actually needed without him having explained it. So, that night, he surprised his partner with a home-cooked meal. They played their favourite vinyl records and shared how they were both feeling.

Through the conversation, Jay fully expressed his vision for their lives and was delighted to hear that his partner was on the same page and committed to bringing back the romance. He also learned that his partner was going through a difficult time with his family, and so was able to give exactly the sort of support his partner needed. They truly reconnected.

Summary:

☐ **The comparison episode was brought about by** jealousy of other couples and feeling neglected compared to the perceived way other couples were acting.

☐ **The crystal of insight here is** that Jay was expecting his partner to answer needs that he had never communicated. As well as this, he was not being the ideal boyfriend either.

☐ **The next step was to act on the insight** by bringing to the relationship exactly what he needed himself – uninterrupted quality time where both people could feel heard and share their needs.

☐ **The change that sticks:** Jay and Scott have one night or day a week where they set aside quality time for each other without fail.

Case study 3: from confidence crisis to a creative career

Sita came to me having a confidence crisis. She had set up her Etsy store a couple of years before and had dabbled in creating, listing and selling her handmade pieces, but hadn't done so frequently. She had taken the same approach with her new company's social media account, which she would post on every now and again. Through her own admission, with life being busy, the online shop and her Instagram account had never really had the care and focus they needed to do really well.

The confidence crisis had come in hard and fast because a close friend from art school had decided to also commercialise her hobby making hand-drawn prints. She had set up an online makers store, with the same popular platform. This was all well and good until Sita found out that her friend was considering giving up her corporate job to work full-time on it. Her artworks were selling like hotcakes and her social media had quadrupled. This apparently overnight success was hard to swallow.

Sita spoke at length and with waves of emotion she found impossible to hold back. At first, she expressed her frustration and jealousy at seeing her old art-school friend sneak in and skyrocket to success in ways that she has not been able to. What followed, however, was the realisation of how much hard work and time her friend had invested, alongside the risks she had taken, in order to build the momentum.

Through further conversation, it became clear that my client had her own appetite to fully commit to her online store and that she actually had a lot of her work sitting about in her studio, ready to list. It wasn't that she couldn't create, it was that she needed to reignite the fire in her belly to consistently support her own art and business. This was her 'a-ha!' moment.

Summary:

☐ **The comparison episode was brought about by** feeling jealous of a friend's perceived easily-come-by success in a field that was too close for comfort.

☐ **The crystal of insight was** that actually she had the ambition and goods available to make a really good go of her online shop and was willing to put the work in, just like she respected her friend for doing.

☐ **The next step was to** book out half an hour every day to work on her online presence and still be able to deliver on her day job, which she was relying on financially.

☐ **The change that sticks:** she no longer feels jealous of her art-school friend. Instead, Sita's glad they have both found their groove sharing and making money through their art, which they are both so passionate about.

You will now be getting a firm feel for how your own comparison complex might operate and how it might have affected your life experience so far. I am often surprised at what a relief it can be to be able to look it in the eye, so to speak. After all, if we can understand our own habits and tendencies, we can work with them.

Perhaps you have lots of triggers or perhaps it's just one dominating trigger. It could be that you now realise, 'Wow! I am really hung up on what my old school pals are doing but I don't give a hoot about celebrities.' Along with this you might also have had realisations about how your personal traits could be assets you are yet to apply, like, 'Hold on, if I put 5 per cent more effort in here instead of being at the beck and call of others, I could see a big change!'

By considering the persona exercise you will hopefully be feeling a bit more warmed up when it comes to the self-enquiry that will be a big part of curing your comparison. Based on the case studies, I would also invite you to start thinking about what crystals of insight your comparison might be holding for you. We will be coming to this in depth shortly, so you don't need to go into too much detail yet.

UNDERSTANDING WHO YOU ARE

'When you know who you are – and you're pleased with
the person you've become – you'll experience a sense
of peace through life's inevitable ups and downs'
Amy Morin

A fundamental part of being more yourself more of the time, and in doing so freeing yourself from your comparison tendency, is gaining a deep understanding of what makes you tick, what drives you and what is ultimately at the core of your being. You know, just casual, right? No, but seriously, this next phase will see you use your head, but also drop into your heart too. We are going to look at some of the barriers to the 'real you' showing up, in a compassionate way.

We will also be introducing you to the wisdom you have within you already, and teaching you how to work with that, staying in-tune with the rhythm of your current life and the road that lies ahead for you if you are able to stay connected with your true self.

What authenticity is

'authentic'
ADJECTIVE
1: Of undisputed origin and not a copy; genuine.

'the letter is now accepted as an authentic document'[9]

If you don't use the word 'authentic' in at least every other sentence, then are you even a life coach?

OK, my tongue is firmly placed in my cheek with that opening line. Seriously, though, authenticity is a word that's bandied about a fair bit, from the self-help shelves to #inspo accounts urging us to BE authentic.

There is such power in the simplicity of the definition of authenticity, and yet it does not really scratch the surface of what it is to live authentically. To go deeper, I believe to live authentically is to demonstrate your values and, indeed, live these by walking your talk with a pure heart, following your legitimate desires rather than copying those of other people. It is through mastering this – living authentically – that we will cut off the oxygen to our comparison tendencies.

To distil this into practical, applicable information as opposed to just theory, I have arrived, through my work, at some frameworks to help my clients and community show up authentically in their lives. The power of this being they are then not tempted to copy others or prioritise someone else's way of being above their own.

You now have the invitation to be and reveal the real you consistently through:

- what you know to be true for you

- how you act

- how you feel

- what you say.

This always feels like a significant part of the client journey as it truly starts to create the shifts towards being less 'them' and more you. We are about to dive into your own authenticity audit and before we do I'd like to highlight a couple of the breakthroughs clients have experienced:

One client realised that they had developed a superiority complex which was leading to them feeling like they had to show off when in certain groups so they could feel like they could fit in and keep up. This was exhausting to carry on, and they realised they could drop the act.

Another became aware that they were a 'goal-post mover', in that they would over promise and over stretch themselves and inevitably end up having to fib and hide the truth in order to try and do what they had said. The 'a-ha' moment was realising they needed to be honest and up front at the beginning so they could go forward harmoniously – no fibbing or emergency back-up plans needed.

OK, let's get into it. For our next awareness exercise, we will reflect and record examples of how you are living authentically. This is also an opportunity to take an audit of how you feel you shape up in each of these categories so you will see a prompt asking you to log a score. Zero is not much at all and there is lots of room for improvement, and ten is a top score and you're absolutely flying your authenticity flag.

1. Being authentically you through what you know to be true for you:

   • I have my own views and opinions, for example . . .

   ....

   ....

   • I know my values and I live in accordance with these. My values are . . .

   ....

   ....

   • 'I see myself neither above nor below others' – is a statement I agree with.
     Yes/No

So, my overall score I'd give myself out of 10 for this authenticity area is:

....

2. Being authentically you through how you act:

   • I can be relied on. Some might say I'm predictable because . . .

   ....

   ....

   • I don't hide things about me, whether on the inside or in my outer appearance, to fit in, for example . . .

   ....

   ....

   • I do what I say I am going to do, for example . . .

   ....

   ....

So, my overall score I'd give myself out of 10 for this authenticity area is:

....

3. Being authentically you through how you feel:

- I trust myself and I have a sense of unflappability, for example . . .

....

....

- I live with a head-and-heart, joined-up approach to my life, for example . . .

....

....

- I don't suppress my feelings, I process them, for example . . .

....

....

So, my overall score I'd give myself out of 10 for this authenticity area is:

....

4. Being authentically you through what you say:

- I know when and how to say no, for example . . .

....

....

- I am always kind even when I change my mind or have to disappoint people, for example . . .

....

....

- I speak the truth and rarely feel called to lie, for example . . .

....

....

So, my overall score I'd give myself out of 10 for this authenticity area is:

....

My total for all four authenticity categories is:

If we view your combined total score out of 40, how did you do? Again this is a judgement-free zone! If you scored below 20 then this is actually really good news as it means there are switches and tweaks available to you now that will help you be less 'them' and more you. You can put your focus on your lower scores and build on what's already there.

If you are coming in at between 20 and 30 then this is also a great starting point. You have some pretty solid foundations in place and with some deliberate focus on some of the pointers you'll be on your way!

If you scored above 30 then I am going to give you a gold star emoji – few people manage to live this consistently so clearly you are already in alignment with what it can mean to live authentically and as yourself.

As there is always room for improvement, let's stay in reflective mode . . .

On reflection, what has held you back from being
authentic in the past?

....
....
....
....
....

What do you feel is holding you back from being
authentic now?

....
....
....
....
....

Based on this, what are some key changes you would
like to make in order to live more authentically? Feel
free to go back to the criteria so you can be as specific
as possible.

....
....
....
....
....
....
....
....

Reconnect with your True You Guide (TYG)

Being the most authentic you is about remembering and removing the layers that your lived experience and environment might have placed over you.

It might feel new, it might even feel scary but the more awareness you bring to this the stronger your sense of self will be, which will power up your own confidence and belief in what is possible. Fear not – this process is not about creating and starting from scratch but rather reclaiming your own inner knowing.

In her book *Playing Big*, Tara Mohr called it the 'inner mentor',[10] those spiritually inclined might label it your 'soul voice', for others it will be described as intuition, gut feeling, true north, inner guidance, guardian angel or God. I tend to call it the TYG (short for the 'True You Guide').

This is the part of you that always knows the answer, without complication. Your TYG truly believes in your skills and resources and your potential to grow, overcome and reshape what falls in your life's path. There is an absence of arrogance when this part of us is leading. We are in alignment with who we are, what we believe and the life we are here to live.

Your TYG truly knows you. It knows what motivates you, your likes and dislikes, who and what you're attracted to, what turns you on, what turns you off, what brings you joy, what makes you feel good, what aligns with your values and views. If we are open to looking, it leaves breadcrumbs for us to follow, orchestrates synchronicities and clears the way of obstacles to what we want and need. Each of us is born with it and as part of this process of curing your comparison, it will increasingly make its presence known or its voice heard.

That said, what if your head feels noisy or crowded because you are feeling stuck in the fog of comparison? How do you tap into its wisdom then? Now, OK, it's not going to email you, so let me share with you specific ways you can connect with this part of yourself even when you are feeling jealous, low or self-critical – this is often when we need it most.

Key to this is shifting your emotional state so you can alleviate the tight grip of your ego that feels like it has you in an emotional choke hold.

Focus deeply on your body and your breathing: Your body's intelligence can cut through the noise of your brain. Taking some big deep breaths all the way down to the bottom of your belly will diffuse the adrenalin sparks that might be firing. Breathing deeply and evenly for 90 seconds can massively shift your physical state and let a sense of calm return to you. Tune into where there might be sensations in the body and ask you TYG what messages these hold – you will be knocked over by what can come through as insight.

Practise compassion for yourself. We are so, so harsh with ourselves, aren't we? Whenever my inner bully voice starts to give me a hard time, I know it's time to turn off the comparison so my TYG can be heard. If you can, take your left hand and place two fingers on your neck and feel your pulse, let your life force tickle your fingertips. Then take your right hand and slowly but firmly rub your heart in a circular motion, which will activate your heart chakra. (Whoah! Did she just say 'chakra'? Yes, she did.) This increases your capacity to love yourself and others and, ultimately, is an incredible self-soothing tool.

Do something you love or that stirs joy within you: Cuddle your pet, FaceTime your lover, give yourself a facial or pedicure, go for a run, listen to your favourite song or poem. It will be different for each of us, but when we are in the grips of ego and fear-driven emotion, it is important to connect with our joy and do something that lifts our mood. It may not banish the difficult feelings straight away, but it will reduce them and from there you can restore and fortify yourself.

....

Action tip: The next time the brain chatter hits or the hot and spikey emotions flare up, dip into your toolbox above – deep breathing, heart chakra stimulation, reconnecting with something that makes you joyful – so you can clear your mind and make space for your True You Guide to come through.

....

As I hope is becoming a bit clearer, the process of becoming #comparisonfree is not only an intellectual one. A compulsory part of my client experience is harnessing the power of our sub-conscious and using visualisation to help us become more in touch with ourselves and our own life path, guided by our TYG. The next exercise will require you to use your imagination and park your purely rational thinking powers. Although these questions may seem a bit 'out there' at first and you might still be feeling twitchy from the chakra reference above, I ask you to go with it and record your spontaneous responses – don't over think it!

Ultimately, we will be letting your TYG bring you messages about who you are here to be and how you can step into that potential right now . . .

- Relax the muscles around your eyes.

- Relax your jaw.

- Let your cheeks feel heavy.

- Continue to inhale/exhale.

- Notice the stillness.

- With each breath, let stress float away.

- Notice your feet – feel any tension or stress come away, feel softness come into your whole body.

- Using your imagination, picture yourself walking down an unfamiliar path. You may not be immediately sure where you are, but it feels good – there is no fear.

- You notice a light in the near distance, it is growing brighter. As you walk towards it you realise that you are actually walking years into the future. You notice that you are going to meet your True You Guide, five years from now. You realise you will soon see a house or dwelling and this is your future home.

- Still using your imagination, you see the entrance of the home come into view.

- Take a look around, what kind of place is this? What does it look like and feel like?

- See your True You Guide coming to the front door to greet you. Take in their appearance and friendly greeting, notice as they take your coat and offer you a drink.

- They lead you to their favourite place in the home for a chat. Ask them, 'In order to get here, what has been most important to you in the past five years?' Your answer might come in words, a facial expression, images, giving you a certain feeling. Write down their answer here . . .

....
....
....
....

Ask your True You Guide: 'Five years from now . . .'

- How do I walk into the room?

....
....

- What do people say about me when I am not there?

....
....

- How do I spend my weekdays?

....
....

- How do I spend my weekends?

....
....

- What am I known for?

....

....

- Who do I hang out with?

....

....

- What clothes hang in my wardrobe?

....

....

- How do I reply to emails and communicate?

....

....

- What words describe my mood and personality?

....

....

- Where do I live? Tell me about it . . .

....

....

- How does my home look?

....

....

- What does my workspace look like?

....

....

- Where do I go on holiday?

....

....

- What do I need to know to get from where I am, to
  where you are, five years from now?

....

....

Now ask them any other question you want their
perspective on, big or small. Write down their
response . . .

....

....

....

....

....

....

It's time for you to come back to the present, thank your
True You Guide for the guidance they have offered you.
Find the path you travelled to get there, coming back to
the present day with each breath you take moving you
further from there, closer to here. Slowly, come back to
your body and attune yourself to the look and feel of
your current surroundings.

This exercise can be really stirring. Before we move on, take a moment to reflect on how you feel about what messages you picked up from meeting your True You Guide.

You may have received very clear visions and advice or there may have been the odd word coming through, or you might have sensed something but felt like it evaded you. Don't judge yourself – you can come back to this part, but log down now what did land with you here . . .

What are your key takeaways from meeting your True You Guide and hearing their guidance from five years from now?

....

....

....

What surprised you about where they were and what they said about your life in five years' time?

....

....

....

What did not surprise you about the meeting? What existing assumptions or expectations were affirmed for you?

....

....

....

....

In our quest to cure comparison and be less 'them' and more you, having a view on what your authentic life – led by your True You Guide - could look like is a valuable one. Especially as through this exercise you have been able to block out the noise of social media and what society tells you what you are supposed to be or what you are supposed to do. The deeply soulful guidance that can come through this exercise may not seem practical on first receiving it but don't worry too much about that at the moment. By the time I have finished with you, your plan and your next right steps will be crystal clear.

Don't give in to the pressure to be or feel amazing

A lot of self-help books and motivational speakers will invite us to dream big and look to create an insatiable appetite for life and all it has to offer. This is, of course, brilliant, and yet do not be pulled into the tyranny of positivity, or the false belief that you have to get on some sort of happy-valley hamster wheel.

No matter what your TYG revealed to you, being joyful and living your life to the full does not mean you need to be skipping through a meadow with dewy skin, wearing Chanel! (Although that does sound amazing, doesn't it?)

After struggling with comparison and its side effects, even feeling neutral is enough of a shift and an improvement to warrant celebration and acknowledgement that you are on your right track. That steady feeling of neutrality shows a calm strength and an inner peace that is like sweet nectar for the soul. It is in that space that we sleep better and can be properly rested, we make better decisions, communicate more clearly, take our time with choices and can both listen and be heard by others because we are in a state where we can do both.

It's OK not to feel the need to climb, strive and hustle if those feelings do not feel authentic or are not in alignment with you at this moment. Their time will come.

In this chapter we have learned how to prioritise our own way of being above that of other people's, in doing so gaining a better view of how we can show up in our lives authentically. This is crucial to successful comparison treatment as it brings awareness to some of the ways we can enable the real us to come through more consistently.

Don't be surprised if the thoughts and feelings from your True You Guide meditation revisit you or pop into your mind in the coming days – this process of understanding who you are can be a very stirring one that will awaken parts of you that may have been ignored or lost until now. This is natural and will provide the perfect foundation for the next phase of the comparison-curing process as we move from necessary contemplation to action.

CHAPTER 3

UNDERSTANDING WHAT YOU WANT

*'I have a deeply hidden and inarticulate desire for
something beyond the daily life'*
Virginia Woolf

Full disclosure, this is not only one of the most significant chapters in the book but also one of the more intense parts of the comparison-curing process. By the end of this chapter you will have an even clearer view of you own personal comparison complex and, crucially, your plan to dissolve it – specific, scoped-out and timed. Yes, really.

So, although you don't need to start doing lunges to limber up for what follows, be mindful that, true to my client programme, this will be an involved and rewarding part of our time together. It's a good excuse to make a cup of tea (but then who needs an excuse for a cup of tea?!).

We will cover how to define your version of success and let go of other people's once and for all. Then we will move onto connecting with your own values and motivations before diving into my signature comparison-curing activity. Following the activity, you will be able to answer the 'what next, then?' question, and you will arrive at your own inspiration toolkit to help you stay motivated and firmly in your own lane (even if you are struggling with wobbly self-esteem). OK, let's get going then – you may as well grab a biscuit too.

Re-evaluating success for yourself

I have a complicated relationship with the traditional definitions of success and how we class what it is to be 'doing well' today in modern society. The classic descriptions boil down to: 'the accomplishment of an aim or purpose' and 'the attainment of fame, wealth, or social status'.[11]

Let's unpick these.

The former description feels pretty accurate, if a bit dry and straightforward. That said, it can apply to so much, and achieving success feels well within reach.

If we connect with that definition, we can be successful at catching our flight on time, successful at going to yoga every day this week, successful at not shouting at our children as often, successful at applying for a new job and so the list goes on. You can be swimming in accomplishments on the daily if we use only that definition as our measure.

The latter, however, feels like a much less accessible, more elitist and narrow definition and it primes us for Olympic-standard comparison to others. By default, it suggests we are unsuccessful if we do not tick those three boxes. If we are not well known, are not a part of the 1 per cent, or we have a lifestyle that does not fit certain socio-economic boxes then it's a case of 'you can't sit with us'.

It makes my skin crawl and stomach turn to think that today, propelled by the pressures of social media, so many of us hustle to 'achieve' these markers when success can be so much broader, abundant and bountiful if we are to think more widely and deeply about what it means for us.

What about having more free time? A better relationship with your parents? A consistent approach to saving money? Being able to contribute more time to your favourite charities? Paying for your wedding without a worry in the world? Being recognised for your amazing problem solving at work? Helping someone less able than you in your community?

Success is not a one-size-fits-all answer or approach

Even though there might be shared goals and overlap between you and other people, success is individual. What keeps me up at night, and what is glaringly obvious from my work, is how many of us sleep-walk when it comes to happiness and fulfilment and how passive we have become.

As The Comparison Coach, a fundamental principle I embed early on with each of my private clients is that:

> *Your definition of success, and your pursuit of it, should present you with broad and deep growth based on who you are and how you want to feel every day. Anything else is at best a compromise and at worst a tragedy.*

Read that again because if you take only a few things away from this book, I need one of them to be this truth as it will continue to serve you as you strive to cure your comparison: success is about you doing you, in whichever way takes your fancy.

An important point to note is, if after reading this book you continue to define your success to include fame, wealth or social status, then all power to you. If, however, you have been spoon-fed that vision without question, I am asking you to check in on whether these measures of success fit you and reflect what truly motivates you. I spent years in the pursuit of 'stuff and status' until a humbling wakeup call (read as: personal breakdown) forced me to re-evaluate what success was and could be for me.

In my late twenties, everything in my life probably looked OK to the outside world but things were very much not OK behind the scenes and in reality. My seemingly glamorous job as a strategist in the advertising industry had me crying in the toilets at least twice a week, my partying was borderline out of control and my home life was about to be turned upside down as my partner and I were losing our house. This saw us move in with my parents for eighteen months – roughly fifteen months longer than we had planned. In case it isn't obvious – this is not the stuff you rush to post about unless you are fishing for a 'U OK, hun?'

During that period, life felt like wading through treacle. We had so much to rebuild and to fix, so many emotional wounds to heal, and yet if there's one thing that will force you to grow quickly and re-evaluate success it is being forced to go back to square one. By relooking at what my own 'wins' were under those circumstances I was able to set myself different milestones to reach to get back on my feet. I had no option but to look at success as a verb – something I had to do and be – as I did my best to build a bridge to something different.

But this isn't my therapy session. I am not here to judge or reprimand you for your choices and aspirations – how ironic would THAT be?! You are allowed to have, and you deserve, nice things and to enjoy OTT experiences! At the same time, you are also invited to audit and decide what these are for yourself, without comparing or benchmarking against other people or feeling like you have to live the dream someone else imagined for you.

Nor do I want you to be hooked on the homogeny of the media image of success, and Instagrammers who are pumping presentations of the same life with a different filter. If we are not careful, success can become too much of a never-to-be-arrived-at destination, reached only through the pursuit of 'more and better'.

When my clients first come to work with me, many of them open our conversations with a long list of what they feel like they don't have – it seems to be a persistent trait of human nature. Most of us come from a place of scarcity when looking at where we are at with our lives right now – what we have not yet done, not yet said, not yet studied, not yet completed, not yet accumulated, not yet ticked off.

The truth is, however, that you are successful right now in a multitude of ways and you can access that treasure trove by feeling gratitude for what you DO have, pride in what you HAVE done, passion to pursue where you WANT to go and appreciation and love for the people in your life right NOW. You are without doubt way further on in your accomplishments than you are giving yourself credit for.

If I ask you to visualise what your picture of success looks like, for you, now, what is becoming clear for you?

....

....

....

How does it feel?

....

....

....

Who is there sharing in it with you?

....

....

....

....

What does it smell, taste and sound like? Let your mind and your heart go wild and write down now how it can be defined.

....

....

....

....

Action tip: Write down a sentence that sums up what success means to you and put it somewhere safe that you can refer to daily. Perhaps stick it to your bedside table, next to your toothbrush, on your fridge, on your bus pass or key fob. Take it everywhere with you!

And to help support you bringing this vision to reality, be aware that there are so many myths and out-dated beliefs when it comes to success. You have an invitation to turn a new page and start defining your own understanding of what success means for you, and take ownership of your trajectory.

Assessing your version of success in real time

When was the last time that you gave thought and consideration to what you want?

What your goals are?

And who you want to be in this world?

So often, comparison thrives within us because we are not aware of our own version of success and how we would like to feel in our daily lives. Many of us inherit our beliefs about success and the roads we think we should take.

This is an important point at which to pause as so many of us think we are failing when actually we are simply not in alignment with what we really want, and we are instead pursuing the dreams and goals of other people. For you, these inherited dreams might come from a parent, a teacher who inspired you at school, or something you heard a friend say once. But ultimately, we inherited that standard or marker of success, we did not choose it and it might have overridden our own internal guidance system.

So, thinking about your work and personal life right now, where does it feel like you are pursuing the goals and dreams of other people? These might be the goals of someone you know who plays a prominent role in your life, or a message from wider society. Journal your answers here . . .

Another pattern I see with clients when they are getting clearer on what they really want is that they have outgrown the goals and desires they once had for their lives. Just like anything organic or nourishing, our goals will often have a shelf life or an expiry date.

For example, you might have set out in your early twenties to climb the corporate ladder and make a name for yourself in a certain industry. However, now you might be no longer interested or stimulated by that work, which would make it time to assess where your next steps can take you professionally. So, let's check in on whether you still want what you think you want.

Understanding what's important to you today

This next exercise will bring radical clarity to what is important to you. This is a compulsory part of the comparison-curing process because when we are clear on our own aligned values, we can work in congruence with them. This allows us not only to make plans, but make choices and decisions that resonate with our values, meaning we are less distracted or influenced by those of other people.

Here is a list of potential prompts that might help you get clearer on your own values:

Peace	Citizenship	Equality
Creativity	Success	Friendship
Authority	Peace	Humour
Knowledge	Justice	Leadership
Beauty	Faith	Freedom
Security	Justice	Fun
Family	Community	Respect
Happiness	Kindness	Adventure

Having mused on the words above, and noticing your own values that perhaps are not featured in the list, let's go deeper and clearly define your chosen values, unique to you . . .

What are the things most important to you in life?

....

....

....

....

....

....

....

....

....

....

What words would you use to describe your values?

....

....

....

....

....

....

....

....

....

Now choose three to five values and expand on what these mean to you. For example, if you choose 'kindness', this might mean lack of judgement, calm expression, compassion, hearing people out, gentleness in communications, generosity in all ways.

1

....

2

....

3

....

4

....

5

....

To what extent would you say you are living these values right now? Sparingly? Or consistently?

....

....

....

....

What do you feel would be the difference to your life if you were living those values every single day?

....

....

....

....

What can you do to live those values more every day?

....

....

....

....

Let's pause here for a pit stop as we are about halfway through the significant part of the process of curing comparison – understanding what you want and through this defining your own success.

Taking the time to arrive at your own values will work hand in hand with the other tools shared this far and will allow you to be and live congruently with what is uniquely important to you.

The intention is you will also be starting to question and take stock of where the temptation to be more like other people might creep into your life – this can sometimes feel a bit mind-blowing so be gentle with yourself as we continue on now.

As you become more familiar with your relationship with comparison, you will use this next part of the programme to build on what has been uncovered and move towards setting your own authentic goals.

Unpick your comparison

This stage of our time together is going to see you complete a far-reaching exercise to get to the root of your comparison complex.

It might feel challenging to start with, so I'd suggest making a cup of tea (yes, another one!), putting on some relaxing music, lighting a candle – whatever makes you feel chilled. Feel free to write in these pages or copy this exercise into a notebook, or, if you don't have those things to hand, use your notes app on your phone to capture your answers.

An open heart, an open mind and radical honesty are needed in order to get the most from this exercise, and if you show up with each of these you will have taken a firm, confident and assertive step towards curing your own comparison. In doing so, you will provide invaluable foundations for the rest of our work together as we head into part two of this book – the Remedies.

First of all, identify and write down in which areas of life you currently tend to compare yourself the most. Below you will find some suggested life areas in which people tend to compare themselves, highlight any that resonate with you:

- Work and professional life

- Love and relationships

- Health and wellness

- Social media following and 'popularity'

- Creativity and expression

- Leadership

- Spirituality and self-development

- Money and financials

- Family

- Home and personal style

- What else? Are there any areas not on this list that are areas of comparison for you?

It might be there are many and varied ways in which you compare yourself, or perhaps there is one hot topic that you simply must crack when it comes to comparison. Your answers to this exercise will be as unique as you are so please just write what feels correct for you.

Now you have identified your own comparison areas, I would like you to choose four that feel most pressing right now. This allows us to prioritise and build awareness so that we can tackle head on those areas of comparison that are the most acute, and, therefore, have the most negative influence in your life right now. You can write these here:

The areas of comparison I would like most to address and cure are:

1

....

2

....

3

....

4

....

Next, at the top of each column on the next page, insert one of your comparison areas and then work your way down the question prompts on the left to capture your own insights about your comparison. It might be worth referring back to the case studies I highlighted on pages 37 to 41 previously as a refresher as I am about to give you the chance to arrive at your crystal of insight.

I have started you off with an example so you can see exactly how to fill out the exercise...

Prompt	1. Yoga training	1	2	3
Rate your comparison score from 0 to 10 (0 is no comparison, 10 is intense and regular comparison).	8			
What was your first encounter with comparison in this area?	Four years ago, when I decided I wanted to be a professional yoga teacher.			
Recall and note down a recent experience of comparison in this area . . .	Last week I saw one of my peers has been invited to teach at a huge exhibition.			
What is your crystal of insight? i.e., why does this trigger your comparison?	I don't put myself out there enough and I want to be seen in the industry.			
What would success for you look like if you didn't have anything – including comparison – holding you back?	I would be more active on social media and would be approaching retreats and events to teach their guests.			
What can you do to reduce comparison by just a point or two?	I can research who is booking the presenters for the Yoga show in summer and contact them.			

Prompt	1. Yoga training	1	2	3
The reasons why you CAN get to your version of success . . .	I know where to find the information. I am a good teacher and I have a lot to offer. The feedback from my classes is great!			
One year from now, what are the things you would like to happen/to have changed for you in this area?	I will have secured 10 guest-teacher bookings. I will feel happy and confident. I will have 10k followers on Instagram.			
What could your halfway point look like (6 months from now)?	I will have a page on my website so people know they can book me for events and I will have confirmed three bookings.			
What can you do within seven days, to step towards your freedom in this area?	I will write my website page and start a Google doc for contacts I can approach.			

Feel free to take a moment and for some deep breaths. This tends to be a really cathartic experience – actually seeing how your comparison has rooted itself, and also seeing the crystal of insight it holds for you and the fuel it can give you, can at first take a while to settle in. So, if you feel you need to take a breather then please do – but you must come back. If you are ready to crack on and further clarify what you want, then let's go, love . . .

Personal clarity with your comparison

Having completed the exercise above, how do you feel about arriving at your unique comparison insights? Write down all the words and phrases that come to mind for you – don't overthink it!

....

....

....

....

What has surprised you?

....

....

....

....

What assumptions have been confirmed/what did you already know?

....

....

....

....

How does it feel to finally be able to achieve some clarity, no matter how small, in this area?

....

....

....

....

What other thoughts or realisations have revealed themselves to you?

....

....

....

....

Self-inquiry is a very new thing for many of us so I ask that you practise self-compassion and not be too hard on yourself as you hold the mirror up to some of your thoughts and behaviours. Even if you are feeling the wobbles of doubt, don't worry. As we work through the book we're going to help you build up your self-belief so that you can come back to this exercise and feel you can get even more clarity from it.

Deciding what we want is not just limited to experiences we desire to have or things we want to own, it can be very much linked to how we want to feel from day to day.

Choosing a compass word

At any time, we have the chance to press reset and line up our focus and efforts to meet halfway what we most want. Key to this, however, is staying really aware of and connected to what you are calling in for yourself. As life is so busy for many of us, it helps to be reminded regularly to act and think in accordance with those personal intentions.

To help with this, I ask clients to choose a word or phrase to guide them, keep them on track and help them stay present. I call it a 'compass word' as it can help them navigate and traverse the conversations, situations and scenarios in their lives that stand between them and what they really want.

It works a bit like a traditional resolution but instead of saying, 'This year I am going to learn to speak French' – highlighting a task – it's more like, 'This year I am going to pursue calm' – highlighting a general feeling. This word or phrase should sum up the feeling or theme you want the year ahead to follow for you. It will help you show up boldly and yet also help with the seemingly innocuous decisions too.

Let me share some examples with you.

My compass word of the year a few years ago was 'consolidation'. That might sound a bit boring and dry, yet back then I felt like I had so many loose ends in my life that I knew a focus on completion and simplifying would be necessary in order for me to show up for my own goals. This was the year that, looking back, my business really took off as all my decisions lined up to focus on it.

The year that followed, my compass word was 'space'. Life was ticking along nicely and yet I felt like I couldn't breathe. I felt cooped in and squashed, both where I was living (working on the kitchen table!) and where my career seemed to be taking me. I knew in order to grow and for my life to flow that I would need more space, so I placed it at a premium. No more cramming in meetings to one day or trying to make working from home my only option. Long story short, I now live on top of a hill and I have all the space I need.

More recently I chose the word 'savour'. This came from a feeling of being spread too thin and yet focusing too much on 'what's coming next?' This word centred me. Whether it's a dinner with friends, writing a blog or hoovering my living room I want to really be all there – to savour it. Not checking my phone, keeping an eye on the clock or checking what's in my diary next month. I want to smell the roses and appreciate everything that touches my senses. I want to savour.

This compass word helps me keep comparison at bay as I am constantly tuned in to my life and my own authentic motivations.

Now over to you, no matter what time of year it is:

Thinking about the next twelve months and what you want them to hold for you, choose your compass word.

My compass word or phrase is:

....

Because:

....

....

....

....

Bringing in this deeply grounding motivation through your word or phrase can help keep comparison at bay in various ways, but most important is the fact that no matter what you see going on around you, it is possible for you to come back to yourself and what is important to you.

Let's continue with our focus on the future you desire to design for your life, based on what you want.

Creating a vision board

I used to love making collages of the things that excited me and that I aspired to. I would have scrapbooks of perfume adverts stuck together and beautiful homes I would dream about living in. On my bedroom walls I would have pictures of the people I admired (Drew Barrymore!) and places around the world I wanted to visit.

When I was a teenager, I guess it looked like a craft project or arty sort of hobby. But I used to look at those images regularly and they motivated me to study and stay positive because one day, I truly believed I could lead that life.

I didn't have a name for it then but now, I realise, I was making vision boards. These are visual representations of your wishes, aspirations and dreams. There are many benefits to you creating your own but the main two are:

- In creating a vision board, you give yourself the time, space and permission to really call to mind what your heart truly desires, free from distraction or complication. It is a sacred exercise as much as a creative one and should be completed with reverence.

- On the completion of your vision board, you have a daily reminder of the things, people and feelings that authentically connect with you and make your heart sing. This provides a daily reminder of what can be in store for you if you keep working on yourself, for yourself.

I like to do a 'general' vision board, which shows words, pictures and phrases that encompass all the different areas of my life to create an overall picture. That said, you could create a vision board around a specific topic you want to focus on, for example, your love life, travel, wellbeing – you name it. The only rules are you have to incorporate what's true for you right now and the #comparisonfree life you want to lead, free from the influence of others.

You can get cracking with your vision board today. I tend to create mine in January and yet, just like a compass word, you can create and activate your vision board at any time and bring into sharp focus what you are working towards (instead of looking at other people!).

It does not have to be neat and symmetrical, but it does have to cram into one space – whether that's a Pinterest board or large piece of paper with cut outs of old magazines stuck on – and make sure to include as many motivating quotes and images as possible.

....

Action tip: Get creative and have fun with it – dream BIG. Create your vision board, whether it's online or a physical version, and tag me so I can be your accountability buddy!

....

Your Perfect Day meditation

If comparison is still making it difficult for you to identify and decide what you really want, this next exercise is going to be just the ticket for you. Again, I am going to ask you to use your imagination and unlock the secrets of your subconscious that might have been hidden away.

In this activity you will be prompted to picture a day so amazing that you could live some variation of it every day and feel, true, authentic happiness. Take a moment to get quiet and allow the visions and answers to flow through you. This is best completed in private, sitting in your favourite place and perhaps even listening to some relaxing music.

Imagine living your ideal day one year from now . . .
Imagine you slowly open your eyes in this perfect day in
your life . . .

Where do you wake up?

....

What do your surroundings look like?

....

What does your morning routine involve?

....

How do you spend the first few hours of your day?

....

When do you start your workday?

....

Where are you working and what do your surroundings
look like?

....

What are the people like you are working with?

....

What passions/skills are you using in your work life on
this day?

....

What kind of conversations are you having around your
work?

....

How do you feel while you dive into this work?

....

When you stop for your lunch meal, where do you eat and with whom?

....

Do you enjoy a long, leisurely lunch or is it quick? Do you cook a meal at home? (Remember, this is your ideal day. It can be whatever you want it to be.)

....

From there, do you go back to work?

....

How do you spend your afternoon?

....

How do you feel as you engage in this part of your day?

....

As the afternoon winds down, what do you do in the early evening?

....

Is this when you work out? Do you meet friends? Go home for family time? What's the ideal way to spend your early evening?

....

Where do you eat dinner and who is there?

....

Do you cook a delicious meal at home, or do you go out?

....

How do you spend the rest of your night?

....

Do you have an evening routine? If so, what is it?

....

How do you unwind?

....

As you get into bed and you're ready to fall asleep, notice how you feel after living this ideal day. What words describe those feelings?

....

Take a moment to review your answers about your own perfect day.

....

What has surprised you?

....

How different is that day to your average day?

....

It may not be possible to activate the circumstances that mean you can start living your perfect day right away and yet, there will be changes you can make, and practices that you can start to adopt now to at least dip your toe in. Perhaps it will also have stirred up some surprising insight about where you want to be.

For example, you might currently live in a remote area, and yet through the exercise you realised that, on an ideal day, you were spending time in the hot buzz of a busy city.

Equally, it might be you are currently single but on your perfect day you are hanging out with your partner you are yet to meet.

These might feel unexpected and yet still aligned with you and the experiences you would like to have, work you would like to do and people you would like to be connected with.

On the other hand, this exercise might have shown you that your perfect day is very close to the life you currently lead but you notice some key differences, such as you have are not based at your desk as much or that you have more time cooking, perhaps you have another dog (winning!).

....

Action tip: Looking back at the outputs of your perfect-day meditation choose one thing you can do differently at one point tomorrow, and then daily, that will move you one step closer to living that life now.

....

Thinking about your own experiences, it's good to take stock and invest the time and focus to define, without apology, what you really do want in your life. And as much as our abilities to visualise will continue to serve us, our dreams and desires need frameworks and a target to aim for. So, let's get into some goal setting unique to you.

Setting goals that light you up today

Let's now look at some practical applications to bring your vision for your life into reality, undistracted by the actions of others.

Making resolutions or commitments to yourself is not and should not be confined to the New Year (although this is a brilliant opportunity to reflect). Your next task is to arrive at your own set of goals so you can be firmly tuned in to your life over the *next twelve months*, letting your TYG lead you.

It might help you to have in front of you the answers recorded for your perfect-day exercise and also the outputs you gathered from your guided visualisation exercise on page 54, where you connected with the you five years from now.

By keeping these previous exercises in mind, you can chart a path back from that future point to today and work out what feels most important in getting you there.

I'm going to ask you now to select the areas of your life in which you feel like you need to set new goals.

Thinking about the areas of your life, which feel most important to allow you to achieve a sense of focus and progress in the coming year?

- Work and professional life
- Love and relationships
- Health and wellness
- Social media following and 'popularity'
- Creativity and expression
- Leadership
- Spirituality and self-development
- Money and financials
- Family
- Home and personal style
- Anything else?

Summary:
The areas of my life in which it feels most important to set my own goals are:

1

....

2

....

3

....

4

....

This starting list gives us a robust selection of areas to inspire the change you want and yet is not exhaustive. You can definitely come back here and apply the insights to more topics down the line if you need to.

Next, follow the SMART goal-setting framework as created by George T. Doran[12] below to arrive at specific, measurable and positively framed commitments.

While there are various interpretations of the acronym's meaning, the most widely accepted is that your goals should be:

- Specific – not 'woolly' or generic.

- Measurable – possible to quantify in some way.

- Achievable – the resources exist on Planet Earth at this time which mean you can attain your goal.

- Relevant – it's aligned with you and your life.

- Time-bound – it has a deadline of sorts for when you will get it done.

For example, a recent client's SMART goal relates to her business. She wants to increase awareness and visibility in her field. So, her SMART goal goes a bit like this:

'By the third week of July, I will have approached twenty journalists with my feature ideas and have a minimum of ten articles published online or in the press.'

Another client's SMART goal focused on their personal life: 'Four months from now I will have moved back home and sold all my furniture and I will be working and saving £200 a month to invest in my travel plans.'

Set your own SMART goals for your chosen life areas:

1

....

....

2

....

....

3

....

....

4

....

....

Your SMART goals do not have to be perfect, but they do have to be yours. No matter how imperfect they might look at the moment, to have them written down is hugely significant as it means you can apply your focus to these rather than to what other people appear to be doing.

A crucial part of working towards reaching these new benchmarks or milestones for ourselves is having the mindset in place to stay motivated and on course.

Changing your beliefs to help change your life

The question is not, 'Is it possible?'

The question is, 'Am I willing to believe it is possible for me?'

One of the toxic things about comparison is it stops us before we even start: 'I'll never be as good/successful/gifted/talented/<insert whatever it is> as they are.' We just plain don't believe it's possible for ourselves.

> *'If you don't change your beliefs, your life will be like this*
> *forever. Is that good news?'*
> – W. Somerset Maugham

This is why so much of my own focus – as well as that of my client work – goes into working on the mindset, thoughts and the beliefs we hold. Now, I know there are all sorts of brilliant techniques that can instantly transform a perspective – Neuro Linguistic Programming (NLP) for example – but my golden go-to process that doesn't wear off has three steps to follow. For some context I have drawn from my own experience in transforming my beliefs around money:

1. **Identify the unhelpful thought**, such as, 'I'm awful with money and I'll never be financially stable. Being wealthy is something that only other people experience.'

2. **Choose a different thought** that you actually can believe and that will 'move the needle' towards a new mindset, such as, 'Every day and in every way, I am getting better with my money.'

3. **Then look for evidence** and gather up those bits like squirrel nuts. Paying a credit card off on time – evidence! NOT going on an online binge to numb my feelings – evidence!

This simple but effective process only works if you follow all of the steps, and yet, it works every single time. I've used this in order to rise up and meet new levels and perspectives in nearly all areas of life. Let's look at this more deeply with further examples:

Current Belief	New Belief
'I will never be able to take care of myself because my life is too busy'	'It is possible for me to make meaningful steps to take care of myself'
'I am too introverted to be successful'	'I can be successful in my own way without following the crowd'
'I will never meet anyone and be in love'	'This is a perfect time to nurture my mind, body and spirit as the time will soon be perfect for me to meet my partner'

Reflect now on your current beliefs in different areas of your life, listing them here . . .

- Work and professional life

....

....

- Love and relationships

....

....

- Health and wellness

....

....

- Social media following and 'popularity'

....

....

- Creativity and expression

....

....

- Leadership

....

....

- Spirituality and self-development

....

....

• Money and financials

....

....

• Family

....

....

• Home and personal style

....

....

• Anything else?

....

....

How can each of these beliefs be reframed to be more positive and motivating for you?

....

....

....

....

For extra credit, write down the changing story as your new choices and facts show themselves to you.

....

....

....

....

OK, let's take a breath! You did it! And if you haven't done it all, you now know what is available to you, so you can act on your clearer understanding of what you want.

The Unpick Your Comparison exercise alone can be tremendously enlightening and, as I hope is clear, you need to be compassionate with yourself as you continue to integrate the insights that you have been able to reveal for yourself. And yet having now accessed my favourite techniques to be more you, such as your compass word, creating your vision board and of course goal setting with your perfect day in mind, I hope you are absolutely buzzing with clarity and ideas about how you can be living more on your own terms.

However you are feeling, look back on your notes before we move on as you will have a picture of your own comparison complex diagnosis and the powers you now have to chip away at it and free yourself from it.

We have completed Part One, so have a gold star and let's turn the key to unlock the next part of your own comparison cure.

PART TWO

REMEDIES

CHAPTER 4

FOCUS

'Where you are right now doesn't have to
determine where you'll end up'
Barack Obama

This chapter and what we will cover next is designed to carve away all distractions that might undermine your efforts to be less 'them' and more you.

Some of these are quick and practical, such as guiding you to assess where your time is actually going so you can gain more back to invest in yourself and what's important to you.

The rest will build on these and provide a turbo boost for your own self-focus, and allow you to get out of your own way so you can zero in on what, when and how to focus meaningfully in your own way. This includes mindset shifts, a masterclass in leveraging what you have and a must-have set of recommendations to quiet all the noise of the of the digital world that can be kryptonite to our focus.

Beware of comparing your current self to your past self

Throughout this process, or perhaps before we met, have you found yourself comparing yourself to your past self? Your looks, goals, possessions, surroundings? I often see posts online declaring 'the only person you should compare to is yourself' and although this is arguably a more positive habit than comparison to others, it's still a sign of disconnection with yourself and an abandonment of who you are. And I'm sorry, love, but I just can't have that on my watch if we are going to cure your comparison. The YOU here today contains untold talents, courage and experience.

YOU in this exact moment, no matter what you look like, are a treasure on Earth, part of the very universe itself in physical form. A heart full of love and strength. Your talents might be weird and wonderful and/or traditional and predictable, but they're talents all the same.

You're complex and difficult to describe because your inarguable individuality means words are insufficient to articulate your YOU-ness.

I'm inviting you to meet yourself here. Right here, where you are today. Having already completed a body of work as part of your comparison diagnosis, it is so important to stay in the present and look at this as a fresh start – an opportunity for a 'do over'.

The fact is, what worked for you in the past won't necessarily work for you now. For example, your body has aged because growing up is a privilege, your family situation might be radically different through gain or loss and tragedy, the demands on your time will have altered and the amount of rest and restoration time available will also have adjusted.

You deserve a fresh approach, a refined and augmented plan to support you, based on what's important now. Enough of yesterday. Take its lessons, gather up its teachings and hold them tight, but do not suffocate yourself by reverting back to what once was. You deserve now. All the days you have lived have led to THIS moment and this phase of your life!

I am not telling you to forget the past and erase the information or clues it holds for you, but do not be beholden to it or let comparison to your past self replace or add to your comparison complex with others!

Dissolving distraction so you can make the very most of your time

Let me be direct with you – talking about time can be a bit dry. This specific subject does not set my soul on fire, but a bit of concentration here is worthwhile as it will allow us to gain back control in this area, reducing the conditions within which comparison thrives. And this is one of the steps of my comparison-curing programme.

OK, with that said, let's get this done! We are continuing with some radical responsibility-taking here. A persistent obstacle to people living fully #comparisonfree is the belief – and often reality – that they do not have enough time to do what they need and want to do. This can be sitting down to write a blog, researching how to set up their Etsy shop, doing their CV, bathing their children, you name it!

Not having time can be an avoidance strategy and it shows that our priorities need looking at. Your goals need you to make time for them if you are going to move forward with them. This next exercise will help you truly understand where your time is going and how you can claim it back.

When you run your diary, you run your life, so let's take a look at where your control might be leaking away. For three days, document how you are consciously and unconsciously using your time and keep a log of where your energy goes. You can copy the prompts below into your notebook, phone notes app or, even better, your digital diary so you can achieve a clear view.

Make notes on how you spend the time, including what you did, when you ate, travel time, where you procrastinated, became distracted, where meetings ran late, your gym classes, traffic jams etc.:

Day:

7 a.m.

9 a.m.

11 a.m.

1 p.m.

3 p.m.

5 p.m.

7 p.m.

9 p.m.

11 p.m.

1 a.m.

Doing this for three days straight is enough time to gain the golden insight it holds for you. For example, one of my clients has three children, so is time tricky to find? Hell yes! That said, through this exercise she realised she was spending about three hours a week watching make-up tutorials. She could have been investing that time in recording her own tutorial on YouTube that she so wanted to.

Another client felt she never had enough time to sit and do admin for her business and it was stacking up. Through this exercise she realised she was going to bed too late, so her mornings were always a foggy, slow start. She set a bedtime and redesigned her mornings to include 45 minutes of admin every day. Calm and efficiency descended!

When you have completed the exercise for a few days, review your goals and values again – set a notification reminder now so you don't forget. You can crack on with the rest of the book with that activity running in the background. You are a multi-tasking genius, after all!

With your three days of data available, next, complete the following exercise to help you reform and refine your daily habits and routines to bring more alignment and balance. (At this point it will serve you to go back to the notes you made in Chapter 3 following your Perfect Day exercise and have these close.) I have included an example to get you going.

The things I will STOP	The things I will do LESS	The things I will KEEP DOING
Stop saying yes to every school helper request.	Avoid getting distracted by Instagram and comparing to others. I still want to go on Instagram, but only as a positive, uplifting experience!	Keep attending my personal training sessions.

The things I will do MORE	The things I will START[13]
Organise weekends / fun things to do with my friends.	Start writing - blogs or the beginnings of a book - just for practice!

I complete this exercise every six months or so to help me reset and re-evaluate where my time is going. I will say that it can occasionally feel a bit confronting to see what habits seem to be more persistent than others. For example, my ever-sliding bedtime, which creeps to be later and later over time (and I then wonder why I feel like I've been dug up some mornings and want to nap by 11.30 a.m.!). On a positive note, however, seeing where I have followed through can really boost my mood, for example, when 'start working out three times a week' moves to 'keep working out three times a week', indicating that I'm sticking to my own wellbeing goals.

This is significant because in this step, to refresh, we are all about building your focus on yourself and a big part of this is understanding how you allocate your most precious, non-renewable resource: your time. Something that those who have cured their comparison have in common is that they choose where their time goes and reduce how it is stolen or sucked away! That said, with life so busy for many of us there are some fundamental first steps we can put in place to set us up for success in this crucial focus-building stage.

Focus in the morning builds focus in your life

Your morning determines your day, so you need to make it count, but how?

Once upon a time mornings were straightforward and uncomplicated. We would wake up, answer the call of nature, dress, have brekky and out the door we would go. And yet, as modern life has developed, mornings have taken on a life of their own – we are checking social media, exercising, attending breakfast meetings, getting kids to early drop-off clubs. It can be a lot.

Here is your invitation to quiet the noise and regain control of your mornings, perhaps for the first time. Introducing mini rituals, practices and actions that will nourish and fortify your mind and spirit, to transform your day and outlook. The blueprint I give clients to trial and adapt includes, as a minimum:

No pre-wee scrolling. Put yourself first and see to all of your needs before catching up on emails and social media in the morning. Be really mindful about when you let those voices into your day.

Shower with the lights off. This is not practical or safe for everyone and yet, being gentle and compassionate with yourself and your physical senses first thing makes such a difference. If you can, wash and get ready in natural light so your senses can gradually start stirring to help you meet your day.

Practice gratitude. Write down five things you are grateful for to give you a little boost and start your day collecting evidence that positive things are happening for and around you.

Listen up. Some of my clients enjoy listening to spa music or a chilled playlist on Spotify to start the day in the most nurturing way possible. If vibrant EDM is your thing, no worries, and yet with a day inevitably filled with stimulus, having even ten minutes of these gentle tones can be incredibly calming.

Considering these recommendations, and the clues from your Perfect Day meditation, design an imperfect, bare-minimum morning routine that you can implement now to set you up to have the best day possible:

A morning routine will set up your day and yet we should be just as conscious of rounding off each day with love and kindness for ourselves too.

Come home to yourself

All too often, on arriving home, the keys go in the door and our attention either turns straight to tasks with a 'go, go, go' attitude, or we simply slump on the sofa before ordering a food delivery.

I get it. Our days can be exhausting. This is all the more reason to give yourself some TLC and extra attention to restore your energy. An evening blue print I share with clients is:

On coming home: put on some relaxing music and light a candle to mark your return to your space.

Nourish yourself. Get yourself a delicious hydrating drink and a snack to give your body a little boost.

Return to gratitude. Again, journal five things that went well in your today or that you are grateful for right now.

Breathe the stress away. Set a timer for two minutes and, with your eyes closed, sitting comfortably, take some deep breaths until the timer beeps.

Relax and reconnect. Next, wash your face and put on some comfortable clothes and take a look at your list of goals. What can you do to move forward with these this week?

> Considering these recommendations, and the clues from your Perfect Day meditation, design an evening routine that you can implement now to set you up to have the best day possible:

Bringing such a mindful approach to this latter part of the day helps you draw back your energy and concentration rather than passively allowing it to deplete. In doing so, this helps you get more, and keep more, focus to invest back into yourself and the people and things most important to you.

Your Sunday service

Sunday night can be really unsettling. You might have partied hard over the weekend and not slept well. Or the weekend might have been perfectly chilled, non-eventful, even, but thoughts of the coming days are creeping in and you are already thinking about the week ahead.

A key exercise I set clients is to design a Sunday routine or excursion that allows them to enjoy that time and stay present for the entirety of the weekend. It also means they are mindful of their time and how to meaningfully use it, again honing their own conscious focus muscle.

To help you harness this special personal ritual, here are some examples of what you could incorporate into your Sunday night routine:

- no social media after 4 p.m.

- cook a meal from scratch and enjoy it with family

- eat at a different restaurant

- walk in nature

- plan something fun to do on your own or with friends

- do a selection of meditations from YouTube

- go to a yoga class

- listen to a self-help audio book

- study something that interests you

- change your sheets

- tidy your bedside table.

The key is to start planning this on Thursday or Friday, before the weekend itself, so it's like an extra bonus to look forward to.

> **Define your own Sunday ritual that you will commit to trying:**

Imperfect progress is really the goal here and for those of us who are parents, carers, travel a lot, work night shifts, etc., you could quite rightly be eye-rolling at this bit. I am absolutely not trying to force on you 'another thing to do' when you are already feeling like too little jam spread on too much toast. I simply ask you to see what could fit for you in the life that you are living right now and make a tweak if you can.

In your own way, becoming more conscious of where you are allocating your most precious resource – time – you can massively increase your own focus. So, get cracking on these awareness exercises as we progress now to another pillar of the process.

Popping the perfection bubble: get out of your own way and give yourself options

So often when a client comes to work with me, they have an awareness that needing things to be 'just so' is sabotaging their focus, allowing their comparison complex to thrive. So, let's look at perfectionism.

A joke I once saw on Pinterest goes something like 'You will know when you are in the company of a perfectionist quite quickly as they will make sure they tell you.'

Although it might seem a bit cheeky, this makes me smile because I have found this to be true on many occasions. And why not declare it? Taking pride in high standards is something to be applauded not criticised, after all, perfectionism can be such a positive trait and can turn things from good to great.

We see it evidenced when we walk into a party and the finishing touches take our breath away and set the scene for a night to remember, it's in the checking of a presentation ten times so that it is word-perfect for that important meeting, it's in the taste explosion of a lovingly prepared meal thanks to the meticulous and time-consuming attention of selecting ingredients.

Perfectionism, on a good day, can make all the difference as it powers the pursuit of excellence. Here's to perfectionists – may we know them, may we be them, may we go to their amazing parties!

And yet, let's not let the nod to the word 'perfect' with its positive connotations dazzle us too much as there is a downside that can be a sophisticated form of self-sabotage if left undetected. Because of the 'all or nothing' mindset perfectionism requires, it can squash dreams, delay plans and keep its proponents stuck in comparison as we see other people well on their own way while we still have not started or have created stunted progress that feels like energetic whiplash.

Brené Brown, an academic and writer, highlights, perfectionism is not the same thing as striving to be your best, rather it is a heavy shield we carry around that we use as a source of protection.

In today's digital age with to-die-for aesthetics and flawless curated content being taken as the benchmark, it is no wonder that more of us than ever are caught up in perfection-driven procrastination. You only have to open one of your apps to see the impeccable poses, unblemished bodies, artwork and sunset selfies that increasingly set the standard for what we deem as the minimum bar to hit. And if you can't hit it, why bother? We feel defeated before we have begun.

Social media is feeding our perfectionist tendencies in ways we have never experienced before, and rather than seeing inspiration on our feeds and following with action, we are over stimulated and paralysed by a fear that keeps us stuck. Like, if it cannot be perfect straight away then what is the point?

This then reinforces the conditions for comparison as we:

- Find it increasingly difficult to be happy for others who are successful as we feel the sting of them being 'out there' in the world doing what we want to.

- Hold ourselves to the standards of others' accomplishments rather than our own.

- Start and make progress on a project and then unrealistically compare ourselves to someone else who might have been working their ass off for years to reach where they are now.

- Become so end-result focused that we skip the steps and flick straight to the end. This means we miss out on the necessary process of learning, finding our own way, and arriving at our own method, our distinguishable tone or look, in the pursuit of reaching our goal, which fuels the fires of comparison even more!

This is all wrong and it breaks my heart to think of the books never written, words unsaid and songs unsung because the obstacle of perfectionism got in the way due to the expectations and standards it inflicts on us.

Achieving success is without exception a process of trial and error and will bring with it numerous false starts, multiple failures and a variety of unforeseen setbacks, but these are often missing from the award acceptance speeches and social-media updates.

Hannah Gadsby, whose Netflix special *Nanette* catapulted her into the spotlight in 2018, has highlighted that success has come at 'such a price'. Her journey included ten years of gigging on the comedy circuit before going viral globally.

Steven Spielberg was not once but twice rejected by the film school at the University of Southern California (USC). Clearly, this was not going to get in his way, however, and Spielberg has grossed $8.5 billion from films he has directed.[14]

Oprah Winfrey was fired from her job on the evening news at Baltimore's WJZ as apparently she was not quite what they were looking for. Looking at the career in the global media she has gone on to build, this seems almost laughable.

Lee Child, the thriller writer, has sold nearly a hundred million copies and counting of his Jack Reacher book series and yet had he not lost his job, approaching his fortieth birthday, none of it would have happened.

Whether a famous face or fiercely private, every successful person has worked to get to where they are and encountered imperfect and ugly moments as part of their journey. Each important undertaking, no matter its size, started with someone taking a deep breath and harnessing their will to try in order to meet the goal or step into their purpose.

So, I guess what I really want to drive home here is don't flatter yourself, you can and must expect some failures and detours on the way to your success milestones. I sometimes have to have frank conversations with clients who think they only want to go after their dream if it's an easy ride, so scared are they of messing up. And yet, what did any one of us do to be set aside as special and put into the fast lane towards our dreams? What makes one person worthy of being singled out to avoid the work, compromise, sacrifice and sometimes pain that we have to show for our efforts?

Nobody gets to skip the work

Your journey will require effort and comprise of twists and turns, but it will be oh so worth it for you. You are off the hook – you don't have to wait for a magic word or a spell to be cast for your dreams to happen, you are just going to have to work for it.

That said, this isn't a trick and there are no baddies waiting to knock you over or pull the rug out from under your feet. You have not been given your unique skills, talents, quirks, opinions, values, thinking patterns and passions by accident. You have not come this far and survived the twists and turns of your path to only then hear an evil laugh proclaim that, 'YOU and you alone are not worthy of what you have worked for – the joke's on you, loser!'

Accept that this isn't a trick.

Perhaps you are going to go all the way.

Perhaps this is going to work out.

Perhaps you should strap in for the most brilliant adventure of your life. I know, right?

Actually getting on with it

Consider this blunt fact: every masterpiece or win that ever was could have been better. The creator, in striving for the very best output or result could have meddled more, agonised over a detail, strategized more, held on to the piece, asked for another opinion. Eventually, though, the time came for Frida to put down her paintbrush, for Muddy Waters to put his guitar away, for Einstein to present his theory.

The time comes when you have to stop and release your work, your art, your idea or your opinion into the world instead of spending even more time and energy in the pursuit of perfect. No more primping, critiquing, polishing or refining. The time for it to be good enough and out there in the world for people to judge and/ or enjoy arrives and we have to step away and release it – whatever 'it' is for you.

'Good, better, best. Never let it rest.
Until your good is better and your better is best'
– Saint Jerome
(Roman-time scholar 347AD–420AD)

Nobody is asking you to compromise your standards, but you are invited to release obsessive control and remain open and unrestricted by perfectionism.

Surely it is better to be on your way and dealing with the comparison that might come up, than it is to have not started and feel the frustration of another person sharing their own thoughts, art or expression when you have not?

In my coaching practice I guide clients to try this 'good, better, best' exercise that will keep you striving to realise your potential, continue to improve and stretch you out of your comfort zone, but detach you from accepting only a perfect outcome.

Take a piece of paper and at the top write down a goal that you want to work towards and achieve. Choose one from your treasure trove you completed in the previous chapter.

Next, write down what would be the perfect and best way you could go about achieving that goal.

Then, what would a 70 per cent achievement look like for you? With you being almost but not quite in reach of the goal, but in a place to stand proud none the less.

Finally, what would be a good outcome? A result that on the surface might be some distance away from your ideal point and yet firmly places you in the ballpark of progress that will deliver you a shift in momentum.

This is your picture of good, better, best. You have just created a scale of success for yourself that provides you with a safe container to take action, measure your own progress and dissolve perfection tendencies that might be keeping you stuck.

This helps us in pursuing our cure for comparison as it allows us to see that any progress is good progress and we are less likely to get hung up on or distracted by what other people are doing. We are all about sharp focus and getting moving at this stage – an imperfect start is still a start!

Learning to leverage

> *'Start where you are. Use what you have. Do what you can'*
> – Arthur Ashe

Ashe was the first black man to win Wimbledon, in 1975, and was also an activist who campaigned for many causes including the fight to end segregation and apartheid and to raise AIDS awareness. I share this because the magic of his words is all too often left without attribution. He was a true change-maker and we should all know his name.

Whenever I feel I am at square one, these words get me going and following the breadcrumbs from there towards the goal that I am working towards. It has also helped me make something out of nothing and stirred up my self-belief, even if a situation had felt previously hopeless. It provides leverage – that is, it allows you to use something, whatever you have, to its combined maximum advantage.

The key to making this advice work is acceptance. This does not mean resigning yourself to, in your opinion, less than the ideal situation. Rather, it's about not dwelling on the belief that things could or should be better for you. This could be true and yet holding on to that will only build resentment and stop you moving forward with confidence.

Start where you are

As much as reflection is incredibly valuable, completing a post-mortem of the mistakes, decisions and wrong turns you feel like you have made thus far is unhelpful. More than this, it's wasted energy that could be invested in what you need to do and be today. Take what serves you and leave the rest. The lessons, insights and red flags are all part of your toolkit to take forwards.

For example, you might have lost your mojo with your career, feeling like you don't have much to show for the last couple of years. Today, take some time to get clear on your personal aspirations when it comes to your work life.

Or perhaps you are healing from a painful breakup and feeling a bit lost and alone. Make the commitment today to work towards reclaiming yourself, journal on your feelings and clear out the painful reminders of the relationship that was never meant to be.

Striving to improve your position in your own way will keep the fire in your belly going, and keep it going you must! After all, as author Karen Lamb highlighted, 'a year from now, you will wish you had started today.'[15]

Use what you have

Someone might have more or better resources, contacts, space, leisure time, experience, money, energy, social media followers than you. This fact has the potential to pull you back into comparison – but don't let it!

So yes, your schedule might be so hectic at the moment that you are really struggling to get the 'me time' you are craving. And yet on your commute, you are just scrolling social media. Instead, download a meditation app and use that time to centre yourself.

You might be drooling over that amazing camera that you know your favourite bloggers use but with finances as they are, it is going to take you time to save up. In the meantime, you can be creative with your smartphone and download some gorgeous pre-sets to your free LightRoom app so you can get your content out there.

The more you put your own resources to work, the more progress you will feel moving forward and you will be more open to opportunities to increase those.

Do what you can

Your own success and happiness will come as a result of your cumulative efforts. Sometimes you are going to have to look at a situation differently to get the result you hope to achieve. This is where stretch and transferability come in.

You could have a new product launch coming up and you don't have a huge online community of potential customers to promote to. But you could write a blog post for an online platform that you know thousands of your ideal customers will read. And you could also ask to go on your friend's podcast that will also increase your reach in a short period of time.

Thinking about your personal life, you could be experiencing a difficult time in your relationship. You want it to work but the arguing is mounting up and the conversations feel unresolved and circular. You can't solve the grievances overnight, but you can research a marriage therapist and suggest it to your partner, so you can bring in the help you both need.

Nothing is ever wasted, so although it might not be immediately clear how to tap into your experience or network of connections, stand back and take a fresh look and remember a scale of options – 'good, better, best' is often available to achieve the positive result that you seek.

Combined, these steps will further hone your focus on yourself and your goals so that comparing yourself has less of a place in your thinking and in how you approach what is in front of you at the moment. Aren't you clever?

....

Action tip: Check in on the goals you set in Chapter 3 and apply these 'start, use, do' prompts from the section above to help maximise your efforts as you work towards those goals. You will be surprised by what other options and routes can be unearthed for you.

....

OK love, we are on a roll now, aren't we? You're reclaiming control of your time, you are more aware of harmful habits and you are clearer on your resources – let the glitter bombs pop! And yet, all this is for nought if we can't get a handle on our online world, so let's dive a little deeper.

Digital diligence to avoid distraction overspill

Although we know that comparison has been with us since year dot, the rise of social media has made it more persistent, far-reaching and deeply rooted in our everyday experience. With this in mind, our powers of awareness and management are being called to come forward and step up in order to reinforce the work and focus you are investing in your offline world.

Many people have chosen to opt out of social media altogether, yet most, regardless of age, gender and background, have some sort of presence that provides a window to the world. It is almost impossible to operate without it and, sadly, there can indeed be a price to pay for not participating ('I want to share your CV for this job opportunity but why can't I find you on LinkedIn?').

We are all at it. OK, you might criticise youngsters today for watching hours of make-up tutorials back to back, and yet you have disappeared down the rabbit hole of an ex-school friend's holiday pictures a couple of times too often and you are not getting that time back either.

In the next part of *The Comparison Cure* we will look to help you find your own formula to cracking the code to a chilled and happy online presence so that you no longer fall prey to the passive time suck.

You don't have to detox

People are often surprised that I advise against a digital detox rather than recommend it. That is, taking extended periods of time offline and away from social media in order to reset and, if you will forgive the language, 'go cold turkey'.

I just don't believe that extremes work in this scenario. Yes, you should not feel dependent on your device, no, it should not monopolise your time and attention. That said, to achieve calm, reduce our stress and increase connection in the real world, the solution lies in changed behaviour and a different approach to social media, not just interrupted use.

Hitting the metaphorical red emergency buzzer could be more of a shock to the system than your current habits and anyway, do you really want to rely on sudden non-participation as a tactic to rebalance your online life? No, me either. Tweaks, refinements and awareness – always, always awareness – can be the difference that makes all the difference. These will ultimately transform our online habits and experiences for the better and to the benefit of everyone around us. For many of us, social media is booby-trapped with comparison triggers and yet we feel lost when we try to work out where to start curtailing those negative aspects.

To make this a smooth, easy and effective practice, I always ask clients to activate my 'house-party rule', that is, if you would not invite that person, brand or account to attend your house party and meet all your favourite friends, eat your food and dance to your playlist on your kitchen table, then they do not have a place in your feed.

Yes, even your sister-in-law, even your pal since school, even the person you sit next to at work. If what they share – which is different to who they really are – does not interest you and/or make you feel good then it's time to unfollow or hide their account for a while. At least until you are feeling like it is the right thing to bring that energy back into your digital front room.

That said, we must beware of the pendulum swing that can come with this. Your reasons can and must be entirely your own when it comes to what to 'dim the light on' but my rule of thumb is that the accounts I follow:

- inform me – 'I did not know that!'

- entertain me – 'I live for these memes!'

- touch my heart – 'See! There IS good in the world.'

- satisfy my curiosity – 'Oh, THAT'S how you do it!'

- inspire my creativity – 'Oh, oh, I can see how that might work for me!'

- challenge me in all the right ways – 'I'm a white, cis, able-bodied, hetero woman and the assumptions I make about the world are often deeply flawed.'

And with all this said I believe this last point is particularly important and we must beware of creating our own echo chambers. That is, feeds full of only people that look like us, agree with us, mirror back to us lifestyles similar to our own.

It is up to you to take responsibility for who you follow and ensure that you follow and include the sources of news, information, activism, non-majority voices, causes and current affairs that allow you to form your own opinions and broaden your horizons and outlook.

Embrace the world around you and educate yourself about the privilege you might have in it, even though it might be extremely uncomfortable. An echo chamber helps nobody, ultimately, and numbing out on only puppies or high fashion in your feed will lead to inertia. To remove every single thing that is not unicorns and rainbows is a pendulum swing too far and denies you your power to be a voice for change and an agency for good in this world.

A feed that actually nourishes you

Let's put the theory into practice and, if it's safe to do so, take out your phone and let's act on the guidance . . .

Open up your social media apps and browse the accounts that are dominating your feed right now. Would you invite these people, brands and things to come to your house party?

....

Mute and unfollow those that would not get an invite and exercise your right to choose.
How did that feel?

....

....

If you were to give your phone to a stranger for a minute, and they were to look at who you were following, would they find a narrow, one-dimensional view of you, how you see the world and what motivates and stimulates you?

....

....

....

....

Thinking about the guidance criteria I highlighted (educates, inspires, challenges, etc.) . . .
What's missing?

....

....

....

....

What is there too much of?

....

....

....

....

So, over to you, harness your awareness to set some conscious intentions and expectations around what your social media world could and should be for you.

What could you be following to bring more positivity, humour, activism awareness, education and cuteness to your feed? Here are some prompts to help you along the way:

Now what? Well, this is the fun bit. You can use hashtags associ-

Work and professional life	What mentors, leaders, innovators, elders and researchers would represent your work aspirations?
Love and relationships	What lifestyles, poets, counsellors, writers, therapists, coaches and bloggers could expand your heart's desire?

Health and wellness	What experts, online voices, bloggers, teachers and trainers can help you keep motivated on your road to self-acceptance?
Creativity and expression	Which artists, wordsmiths, thinkers, writers, essayists, performers and actors can stimulate your creative spark regularly?
Leadership	Who are the thought leaders, best-practice makers, original thinkers, praised practitioners that can help you rise up to meet your leadership potential?
Spirituality and self-development	Where can you find content on belief systems and philosophies, astrology, meditation and mindfulness that can answer the needs of your spirit?
Money and financials	What brands, people or organisations can help you to work towards the income, savings, debt management and investment goals you hold?
Family	What communities exist that can meet you with the support and empathy that will serve you right now, no matter your age or life stage? E.g. fertility, wedding planning, bereavement.
Home and personal style	Who can you follow to help you express yourself through fashion and interiors, whether that is seasonal trend-led or #slowliving?
What else? Or something different?	Do you have any forgotten hobbies or sports interests? Perhaps you love a certain comedian or are just absolutely obsessed with a place in the world? Get it in your feed!

ated with each of your own answers to find and follow the accounts, voices and people that will fill your digital dance floor. You can also ask for recommendations from your friends and online pals for their top tips. From here it is up to you to tweak and refine accordingly over time.

....

Action tip: Start using these hashtags in your social media posts to show your participation and tag me @lucysheridan in your posts so I can see your house party.

....

How we participate online will be down to each of us as individuals. As our everyday lives can be busy and over-stimulated, the last thing I am suggesting is that you start commenting and leaving emojis on every single new post that starts to light up your app. That said, expressing your own thoughts and saying when you appreciate something someone has posted can bring a real positive spark to social media.

I get that those who identify more as introverts might cringe at that thought and yet, the way I see it, to be silent and just lurk on social media is a bit like flicking through a magazine passively. Yes, you get a moment of stimulus, but delving in can be such a rich, vibrant experience and is a gateway to finding more of your people.

Bringing our consciousness to what we allow in our feeds and how we feel about that content can not only help us stay focused on our own path and on what inspires us, and also help us rise to the challenge of being a force for good in the world.

Unfollowing further helps your focus

If ever there was a subject that epitomises the problems we are encountering in this, the awkward toddler phase of social media, it is the concept of unfollowing. Since when did the tap of a button become so significant? Ever since we decided to give it significance.

It is really important to highlight that whether you follow someone on social media, or indeed whether they follow you, is little or no reflection of your real life connection and measure. For example, I don't follow a friend of mine's social media account documenting her house renovation because I do not give one single duck about how that is going, what it's costing or whether the paint is drying.

And yet, will I be there with a bottle of champagne in each hand to enjoy her house warming and congratulate her on her hard work? You bet your bottom dollar I will. And before then, am I FaceTiming her to ask what she wants from the takeaway before I turn up to her building site of a home, because I know she's too busy to cook and grout the tiles at the same time? Damn straight I am! But do I follow her on social media? No. And that's OK.

And it goes both ways. I know several – putting it modestly – friends of mine that have unfollowed, hidden and blocked my account(s) because they just don't want the topic of comparison popping up in their feed every day. And yet do they flood me with emojis with wishes of good luck before I do a talk and shower me with good vibes when they see me hit a business milestone? Yes, they absolutely do. Wild horses could not stop them. But do they follow me on social media? No. And that's OK.

When someone unfollows your social media account it is not a withdrawal of support, nor a syphoning away of love and appreciation for you and who you are. The more we start understanding that fact the easier it will be for everyone. It lets each of us off the hook.

I want you to remember this the next time you notice a name absent on your followers list. And, equally, the next time you second guess whether to unfollow an account so that you can have a bit of a breather while you recoup and replenish your own self-focus and individual motivation.

But then, what happens when you go to follow the person again? I know this might be filling you with a tinge of fear.

This is easy, and in fact, let me save you the trouble. Here are the exact words to handle it, which I have used countless times before:

> (them):
> *'Hiya, I've just seen a notification/request from you? Did you unfollow me? Is everything cool between us?'*

> (you):
> *'Hey, yeah, I am following you again. A little while ago I had to take a bit of space on social media as a few things were triggering me. But I am back now and I can't wait to see your posts – your holiday looked amazing (or insert other observation). See you soon, I hope! <insert emoji of your choice>'*

Note some key elements of your response:

1. You acknowledge that you unfollowed.

2. You share your point of view without superfluous detail or a multi-paragraph rundown of what was going on for you.

3. You do NOT apologise.

4. You leave it with a positive feel and move on.

. . . .

Action tip: Start to flex your mute and unfollow muscles

on your social media apps, safe in the knowledge that you
have the perfect response on the rare occasion you might be
questioned about it

Here is the thing to remember when you are dissolving comparison in order to focus on yourself – you do not owe anyone your
attention. Nor do you owe them an explanation. You are not here
to convince or persuade anyone of your reasons because they are
just that, *your* reasons. Nor do other people need to account for
themselves.

Our individual mental health and emotional stability trumps
seeing Susan's before-and-after pics – sorry, Susan!

Don't let the filter factor mess with your focus

> *'Don't trust everything you see . . . Even salt looks like sugar'*
> – Maryum Ahsam

Oh boy, have I been tangled up in this before. Making assumptions and with those fabrications creating a stick to beat myself with.

'She has eight children and still manages to have perfect hair!'

'They have just started out and suddenly they have a huge social
media following!'

'How it possible that they are on another romantic trip? They just
got back from one!'

What we see is often a curated and consciously presented version
of a truth, not the unfiltered sharing of the truth. And before we
get caught in an 'us and them', holier-than-thou mindset, let's be
real that each of us participates in our own individual fame bubbles.
I know I do. It is not uncommon for me to reach double figures trying
to capture the perfect selfie. Or when asked to be in a picture, pose
as if I'm in front of the media at the Oscars when the reality is I am on

my friend's garden patio in Yorkshire sipping lukewarm rosé.

That said, we are only human, and it can be irritating to perceive people faking their reality to look a certain way, or be seen to live a certain lifestyle in an attempt to claim status or collect likes. Some people take an online persona to an extreme and that's when sometimes we need to press mute, hide or unfollow in order to preserve our offline, 'real' relationship, without any of the filters or out-of-character comments.

So, I guess it is fair to say that not everything is as it seems . . . apart from when it is. Let me elaborate and, fair warning, this next bit might be difficult to swallow when you contemplate applying this to your comparison trigger who comes over as the smuggest person on earth. They may have good reason to be smug.

The fact of the matter might be that for every person that is augmenting and enhancing their reality, there is someone else who has nothing to hide and their life really is as shiny behind the camera as it looks on their feed.

They are that happy post-divorce.

They really have landed a special opportunity in their work.

They really did find it easy to get pregnant.

Their house renovation really has gone smoothly and with the stunning results on show to boot.

And that is OK. We will soon come to explore the fallacy of the zero-sum game, that is, a win for another person equates to a stolen chance from you.

We must do our damnedest to let others live and grant them the same support that we would want to come our way when our 'woohoo!' moment lands with us.

It can feel unfair, sure. And yet if we are paying that much attention to what someone is doing then our internal warning lights should be flashing as we have swerved out of our own lane – we are in the grips of comparison.

Now, OK, we may not be ready to wish them well or send them flowers, but we can't accuse them of being liars either. How annoying! Just like the results you create and the changes you make in your own life are real, so too are other people's.

Online hacks for inner peace and further focus

The approaches shared up to now can and will ensure we no longer feel trepidation or at the mercy of what we see on our feeds, which further reinforces our own clarity. To add to this, there are some other areas we need to ensure we have covered in order to promote a happier, more aligned and abundant online life.

It does not begin and end with managing our social media wisely, although that's a big part of it! These other tips and techniques below will start to strengthen the protective boundaries around your time, attention and energy so that you can invest these back into yourself, your goals, and the most important people in your life.

Put an out of office message on at all times. Everything feels sort of urgent even if it isn't proper urgent these days, doesn't it?

We have come to expect immediate replies and it can feel impossible to accurately prioritise our communication and consciously invest enough considered time and thought into what we want to say.

By buying into the myth that there is a premium on immediacy, we promote it and in so doing, the vicious circle continues. We 'fire off emails', 'quickly ping over the info', 'jump on requests', in order to 'keep on top of' our inboxes. Even the language feels a bit manic and combative, and at what benefit to us?

Fair enough, in a work environment we have to help out our colleagues and when a situation calls for it, rush to meet deadlines that have perhaps been moved or forgotten. And fair enough – I don't have much time for pleasantries and small talk when I'm stressed either!

And yet, with only finite waking hours in the day – and with your intention to regain power and control over your time, focus and energy – if the email can wait for a bit, let it wait for a bit.

This is where the permanent out of office message comes into play in order to:

- manage the expectations of the other person

- allow you to respond properly (or not at all in some cases)

- tell the world you're in charge of you

Again, this may not be possible to apply for work emails but it can be put in place on your personal email account(s) and you will find it immediately makes you feel better. For entrepreneurs and self-employed people, I would also recommend this on your primary work email account.

The message can be a simple as this:

'Thank you for your email. I check this account a couple of times a day/week and respond to urgent messages first. With my life feeling particularly vibrant right now, thank you for your patience if my response is not immediate – I really appreciate it.'

The race to zero. And while we are at it – let go of the coveted 'emails at zero unread' status of your inbox. Having no unread email does not necessarily mean you are super productive and efficient, it often just means you are really good at writing lots of emails which, spoiler alert, is not something that someone will reference as a key attribute in your eulogy.

I had a client nearly break out in cold sweats when the homework I set her from our session was to check her personal emails only twice a day for ten minutes at a time. On regrouping for her follow up she told me that yes, she had unread and unresponded-to emails but all matters that needed her attention were seen to.

She had also been present for every bathtime with her children and had refurbed an old dresser she had inherited because she finally had the brain space to start chipping away at her real-life jobs she wanted to move forward with because she had stopped treating herself like a bot on an electronic help desk.

Turn off blue ticks . . . in fact, turn off all notifications. The blue ticks reference here relates to the 'received and read' status on WhatsApp. If you spot those blue ticks on the instant message you just sent then you know that person has safely opened and digested it. Or have they?

I believe blue ticks mean nothing. If I am checking my phone while I am about to board a train and I happen to click on your message by accident, you can be sure I have absolutely not digested the message. So cool your jets if there is a delay in my reply – I am just out here living my life, trying to catch the right train at this moment.

We check our apps so very much that I would actually invite you to consider whether or not you need any notifications on at all?

By turning off prompts and notifications we can become more conscious of when we are present online and eradicate the damage of the regular, minor distractions that can pull us off task so many times a day.

Side chats and splinter groups for focused friendships. One of the best things about the internet is it allows us to be switched on and connected no matter our time zone and/or stage in life. The group messages and emails can, however, be overwhelming and oftentimes feel like a bombardment of irrelevance. There! I said it!

It might be it's a WhatsApp group with family members discussing plans for a festive get-together . . . but it's only July!

Or former colleagues of yours that stay in touch with each other through a daily ebb and flow of updates from the sublime to the ridiculous.

Perhaps there is a group trip around the corner and a couple of people are faffing around with their own travel plans, feeling the need to share the minute details.

Whatever the situation is, needing alone time and avoiding big groups is not just for introverts, especially when you are building your own self-focus. Ensure that if you are in a group you have given permission to be added and if you need to mute or exit, that you do so. Our relationships online are much calmer when the energy and exchange are properly channelled, reciprocated and managed.

So, if in reality you are only close friends with a couple of former colleagues and the others are just not your people, hold on to those contacts and with kindness remove yourself from the others.

We have all been there! Feeling a bit fed up and frustrated with the endless updates, especially as one side effect of this is FOMO (the Fear of Missing Out).

It is easy to slip into comparison when we see the pictures shared from that night out we could not attend, or perhaps that function we were not invited to (awkward!). If we are not careful we can start to question what we were doing instead of going on that night out, our choices becoming overshadowed by what our friends are doing. But don't take the bait! Staying aware of when these triggers come up is part of the process, you will find as you go that these derail you less and less. Ooof, what a relief.

....

Action tip: Start to trial the digital-management tips above and keep the ones that work for you. Through implementing these we put the world at arm's length and create the room we need to keep working on the goals that matter most to us, all the time decreasing our comparison through investing in ourselves.

....

It is not, however, only our online lives that need some sweeping and polishing. Our real-life living spaces need a bit of focus too, if we are to stay truly connected to our own lives.

Make space for your future

My name is Lucy Sheridan and I am an emotional hoarder in recovery.

It was only a couple of years ago that I finally started having regular clear outs of my stuff that up to that point I had been resisting. It had become impossible to ignore the fact that holding on to the past was complicating and holding me back in the now.

I feared the emotional pain of having to let go of mementoes, trinkets and nostalgic items, having traditionally attached a lot of meaning to *things*. My college bus pass, birthday cards from my teen years, cinema tickets and travel itineraries from previous relationships, payslips from my first jobs . . . you name it, I had it all hoarded away. And with it came the emotional baggage and clutter that was taking up space in my mind and heart too.

Back then, this fuelled my comparison tendency as it kept me feeling stuck and comparing myself to people who seemed to be able to have a smooth and spacious home life. On top of this, it affected my focus because how can ideas and action flow freely when they are surrounded by piles of laundry and dog-eared photographs?

In this Marie Kondo-aware age of 'does this spark joy?' we now better understand why it's important to strip away the clutter to create a calm and flowing space in our homes – and we have more tools to do this – but that doesn't mean it is any easier for some of us.

My resistance was rock solid. In my head, my clear out would mean me crying uncontrollably at the end of my bed, surrounded by rubbish, and I just wasn't prepared to put myself through that. Until the time, that is, that I realised my attachment to possessions, and with that certain periods of life and the people in them, was interrupting my relationships in that moment, which could threaten my own #comparisonfree future.

It was the steps I am about to share with you that meant the inevitable clear out I needed to complete was not as painful as I thought it would be, nor was it the long and gruelling process that I had expected either.

If you know that you are snowed under with junk, clutter and stuff that doesn't serve you now, nor will it help you grow into the person you are here to be, here are my three golden rules to let go of the emotional baggage once and for all:

1. **Commit to it.** Making space, and with it, clearing energy, takes time. On embarking on my clear out, I blocked out a weekend in my diary so I knew it was coming up and it would not budge or be delayed any longer. I said 'no' to social invites and decided to use the time to the fullest. I also imagined how amazing it was going to be to wake up on Monday, after that weekend, and see my sparkling, clean new surroundings.

2. **Send thanks and forgiveness to the items and people associated with them.** Having set the date for the clear out, I needed to take the edge off my emotional reaction by allowing myself to process the feelings that had started coming up. This was about making peace for me as much as about creating more room in my house. I started sending love and forgiveness to the things I knew I was getting rid of as well as the people associated with them. How? I literally visualised pink and gold light being sent like a laser from my heart to theirs and repeated in my head 'I reclaim myself and let you go'.

   For example, in meditation, or just when I was walking down the street, I started saying goodbye to the time my ex-boyfriend mistreated me, or the friends I felt had wronged me in the past. I gave thanks for happy times with loved ones that had passed away. I nurtured my inner child – seventeen- year-old me – who was heartbroken and confused, and I was holding on to so much from that time.

   This allowed my feelings and memories to start moving, having been stagnant and stuck before I actually approached the items with a bin bag. I was able to meet and walk through those emotions gradually, over time, rather than have to face them head on in one go.

3. **Keep focused, knowing the rewards are on the other side of the clutter.** I just could not bear the thought of sitting

at the doors of my wardrobe, deciding whether I loved a
broken flip-flop or not. I knew this was not going to serve
me. I needed a more surgical and forthright approach in
order to 'cut off the leg to save the body'. If you can see an
overstuffed envelope of old birthday cards, do you really
need to read every single one? Probably not. Put them in the
recycling pile quickly. Be assertive in service of your healing.

Ultimately, how much space we have for ourselves influences how
much magic we can call into our lives.

You could live in a mansion and still feel like you have no space,
or you could live in a studio flat and feel like you've a real abundance
of space. I knew that in my home at that time I was holding on to
possessions that were stopping the things I wanted coming into my
life.

For example, how could I ask for more love from my husband
when I still had a pile of love letters from ex-boyfriends? It made no
sense, which is why I was so ruthless about really paying attention to
not sending mixed signals to the universe.

The result for me, and for the clients that undertake this task, is
a sense of pressing 'reset'. Bringing awareness to what we actually
need and like to be surrounded by means a more supportive home
life and an environment where you can work on yourself, for yourself.
This further helps our self-focus because we demonstrate we are
showing up for ourselves, and who has time for comparing when life
is moving and flowing?

You might have noticed that one of the subtitles of this chapter is
'Actually getting on with it', and that really is key to achieving focus.

Arriving at your own special mix that dissolves distraction will
most probably be a process. And yet, I hope that having gained a
clear view of where your time has been going, and becoming more
conscious about the dynamics of your digital world, you are able to
start making some priority changes now.

Another key takeaway from here is uncovering what might be
available to you now to act on and truly leverage your present

position, so do look at how this can work with the goals you set towards the end of the previous chapter. And if the thought of taking action and getting going is bringing some butterflies to your tummy then don't worry at all – we are going to cover this in our next cure for comparison: building self-confidence.

CHAPTER 5

SELF-CONFIDENCE

'The worst enemy to creativity is self-doubt'
Sylvia Plath

One of the pillars of this next chapter is the concept that your confidence is defined by you. What a relief! So many of us compare our confidence and how we strike out in the world (or not) to that of other people. We perhaps feel like we fall short in this area, despite what it might look like to the outside world, which can directly impact our ability to show up for ourselves and act on our new-found focus.

With that said, to help you honour and grow your confidence supply I will share with you some key pointers that can activate your existing source and create momentum and the results that are most meaningful to you.

It is a good idea at this stage to review the goals you set in Chapter 3, as what follows here could stimulate some new ideas and options to gain even more progress.

The fear of success and how it can affect you

Some words of warning are necessary here, if you are to go all the way in curing your comparison. We will explore this area and the tools available to support you throughout our time together – I have got your back. And yet, because I know this programme so well, I need to share with you an unexpected obstacle that about 80 per cent of people who follow these methods experience when things start to go really well, thanks to their new-found focus.

So many of us are completely untrained in how to deal with success and happiness in a consistent, long-term way. There are certain fears that are going to start to rumble as your commitment to yourself starts to create results, and these should be anticipated if they have not shown themselves before.

In *The Big Leap*, one of my favourite books, Gay Hendricks highlights the hidden barriers to success as follows:[16]

Feeling fundamentally flawed. This comes up because deep down you have a feeling you are not really deserving or worthy of the life you dream about. So, thinking about actually achieving your dreams might make you feel wobbly – like you want to cower and recoil.

Disloyalty and abandonment. You might have this fear if you are worried that expanding to the size of your goals and achieving them will not be approved of and might lead your loved ones to reject you. It could be you know your family have a bitter dislike for a family member that has 'made it' and you don't want to end up an outsider like they have.

Believing that more success brings a bigger burden. Because of sayings like 'more money, more problems' and 'no good turn goes unpunished', you might fear that achieving what you desire will mean more and different problems for you. There might be a belief that ungrateful, slimy people will 'come out of the woodwork' and bother you.

The crime of outshining. This is so widespread – it's the belief that to be successful is to make others look bad, hurt their feelings, and equates to hogging the spotlight. This can be traced to child-hood for many of us: 'Don't tell your sister about your exam score – you know she isn't doing well at school at the moment.'

If you were to be really honest with yourself, to what extent have these fears cropped up for you? Some of these might feel completely new and yet others might resonate with your own beliefs and experiences. Knowledge is power, so to bring your awareness to these is already a bit of a win in our quest to cure comparison.

What will help us overcome these fears, however, is feeling like we can step assertively towards the life that we want to create and experience. A significant part of this is building and sustaining our confidence levels.

What is self-confidence?

Self-confidence is a deep knowing of yourself and assurance of your abilities, resources, potential and personal judgement. It gives you agency in your life and allows you to harness and grow your inner power.

A self-confident person, often without shouting, or needing to declare it, exhibits their abilities in a natural and effortless way. They don't tell people who they are, they show people who they are. The life they lead and the relationships they have speak for themselves. Perhaps they make it look easy, but the reality is, like anything worthy of cultivation, it takes time.

There are individuals that seem to have been born with a bounty of the stuff, but through my own research I know they are certainly not the majority, and those who possess self-confidence and enjoy its benefits have each had to crack their own individual code. This provides hope for us all, whether you were raised by an outgoing beacon of enthusiasm or your caregiver was very much a glass-half-empty kind of person.

Confidence is not an inherent attribute or a permanent, guaranteed state, no matter how unflappable you believe someone to be. It's fair to say that some people are born with more of the stuff than others, but most of us will need to work at it.

Even your best mate that always knows the right words to say is nervous about getting back in the dating game after their break-up.

Even your creative pal struggles to show up for their writing because they don't believe what they have to say is of worth.

Even your sibling that laughed off that minor car crash at the time, now dreads driving and struggles with anxious feelings.

A life event or a negative mindset can wobble and topple the confidence of even the most capable, bright humans.

On any given day you will be standing somewhere on the self-confidence scale, scoring yourself anywhere from one to ten, with one being when you are feeling low and vulnerable (when you find yourself hugging a radiator) and ten when you are feeling unstoppable, with your heart bursting out of our chest (think about when you get a text or call with the news that your hard work has paid off and you feel pumped up and proud of yourself).

Self-confidence helps to cure comparison

Boosting your self-confidence is a key step in ridding your life of comparison as it gives you agency over your actions and ownership of your thoughts and behaviour. It allows you to leverage your own resources, no matter how plentiful or scarce they happen to be, and it ultimately allows you the impetus to use your inner power to work towards what is important to you. Without self-confidence, words go unsaid, ideas undeveloped and your time is often spent on the wrong things, with the wrong people, because we feel too scared to make a change or we hope the change will magically make itself. This naturally leads to a growing sense of discontent and in those conditions, comparison thrives, and the vicious circle continues.

And yet, when we activate our self-confidence, we can immediately create positive shifts and deliver on the promises we have made to ourselves and those we care about the most. Think back to Chapter 3 and the Unpick Your Comparison exercise that you completed. There's a good chance that your perfect scenario in step four included a sense of belief, self-esteem and trust in yourself and connection with your own goals.

I want you to have these specific exercise outputs in your mind as we complete the next part of The Comparison Cure – refer back to them now if you need to. This is all about you and I want your focus on your own heart's desire to be front and centre throughout.

Your comparison complex can't thrive when you take responsibility for your confidence, as it will not have a leg to stand on.

For me, confidence is not something you are, it's something you have and just like a supply of anything, one day you can be up and the next you can be down. So, if you find your self-confidence feels inconsistent or changeable, welcome to the human race because it is. Go easy on the self-judgement and meet yourself where you are today so you can understand your current supply of confidence and what you can do to replenish, promote and protect it.

It helps me to look at self-confidence like fuel in the engine of life – the more I have, the further I can go and the longer I can drive towards my own goals, whether that be professionally or in my personal life. That said, even though I would describe myself as confident on the whole, I can still catch myself on the verge of an existential crisis, sliding down the wall crying and wondering what I am doing with my life, feeling like I have zero self-esteem. I feel like a squeezed lemon. Nope. I'm done. These feelings can last for an afternoon and then they are forgotten, or they can take up residence and stick around as uninvited guests that just won't leave, and I'll need to cancel any and all plans and promises so I can come back to myself and work up my confidence muscles.

So, this brings us to your next assignment. Rather than just *being* confident infinitely and with no ebb and flow, it's up to you to leverage where you are and create the conditions for your self-confidence to dwell and thrive within you. We are going to start today to cultivate our awareness and efforts to support this intention.

Before I take you through the specific keys you can choose and use to build your own self-confidence supply, let's just acknowledge that this is a sensitive and emotive topic.

Take ownership of what confidence means for you

So many of us have a complicated relationship with confidence and this is most likely because of what we have observed in the behaviour of others or absorbed from messages in the media, so let's clear up some of those myths now.

Perhaps when you think of what embodies self-confidence this brings to mind people you know that have gone after what they wanted at any cost and trampled on others along the way. That's not confidence, that's ruthlessness.

Or what about that loud OTT friend you have that speaks over other people in order to be heard or to stand out in a crowd? That's not confident behaviour, that's insecurity.

And then think back to that boss or colleague that has an unhealthy drive to be seen as the best and hold on to their perceived position in the lead. That's not confidence, that's narcissism.

These are just a few examples that might resonate with what you have believed to be a function or requirement of confidence, and yet, we've mistakenly labelled it so many times.

I'm inviting you to appropriate it for yourself, starting now.

What does confidence mean
to you?

What words or phrases
define it for you in your life
right now?

Where might there be some
confidence gaps to plug in
your life?

Who do you feel is a good
example of authentic
confidence? And why?

And now we can go even deeper. Amazing confidence levels are not just going to happen overnight, but you will be surprised how one decision can make such a difference in the short term.

Each time you make a different call for yourself it's like turning the key and you are rewarded with even more confidence. It's a series of conscious decisions that will be the difference – that makes *all* the difference – and this is where the next comparison-cure exercise comes in.

Below are my keys to confidence for you to digest and then interpret and activate in your own life. I categorise the ways we can build our confidence into sets that I have found work well for my clients and can be adapted for you as an individual, specifically:

1. Confidence through your words

2. Confidence through your approach

3. Confidence through your actions.

1. CONFIDENCE THROUGH YOUR WORDS

a) Speak your truth, and prepare with notes

Many of us would rather stay silent than say what's really on our minds. We worry about how we might rock the boat, cause or participate in conflict. There comes a time in our lives, however, when we don't get to sit it out or avoid it. It's necessary to deliver serious, significant and sensitive information to others and an email is not going to do the job.

In so many areas of our lives, doing the right thing calls for us to be kind and confident. It might be ending a relationship, leaving a job, having a difficult conversation, backing out on something you had previously agreed to or simply giving some feedback. Whatever the scenario might be, this is the perfect opportunity to show up for yourself and work your confidence muscle to the benefit of your own goals and motivations.

My first piece of advice is that the first time someone hears it should not be the first time you say it. So, when the time comes for you to speak your truth, ensure you practise whenever you can. In the lift, on the train, in front of the mirror brushing your teeth – do what you can to become familiar with your words, so you do not trip over them.

Often, we simply cannot control the outcome, and yet we can influence a good one if we put thought into how we show up for the conversation. It will not always be possible to have lots of preparation time. And yet, the more time you do have and use, the better you'll perform when an ad-hoc or reactive response is what is asked of you.

....

Action tip: The next time there is a challenging conversation to be had, make a few notes that highlight the points you need to deliver, then formulate your opening and closing words. Practise in the time available, to improve a smooth delivery and, crucially, increase your confidence.

....

b) Personal pep talks – be your own cheerleader

It's such a thrill to get an email of thanks from a colleague or a high five from a pal that believes in you and can see the work you're putting into being your best self. It can give us the warm and fuzzies even thinking about the bonds of appreciation we share with those in our circles.

That said, few of us actually wake up to encouragement or pats on the back out of the blue from the people whose opinion we care about. The reality is, nobody will DM you before that big work meeting, there won't be a bunch of flowers to congratulate you for ending a toxic friendship and you're not going to receive a social-media shout out for going to the gym like you said you would.

Most of the time it's crickets and tumbleweed on that front so we need to actively play that role for ourselves and be our own best friend. Just because the actions and decisions we take for ourselves might be small, the fact they move us towards our own version of happiness makes them valid, significant and worthy of acknowledgement and appreciation. So, give the positive re-enforcement to yourself as often and as specifically as you can.

On days where my confidence might be low and I'm feeling vulnerable my words to myself become kind and compassionate and I'll rub my heart and repeat, 'You're safe, you are loved, you are doing your best. Be gentle, babe, be gentle.' This has an immediate soothing effect and from there I can regroup my thoughts and look to finish the day on a positive note.

My personal practice depends on how I'm feeling. If I have a full confidence tank, my personal pep talks might be as simple as, 'Well done for not sending that bitchy email – you're better than that and it shows how much you've grown.' It's in these micro acknowledgements that we not only know the progress we are making, but we can feel it too, and it's heaped on the growing pile of evidence we can trust ourselves and our decisions, which amps up our confidence.

Action tip: Set the intention to swap the bullying or critical voice in your head for a champion and cheerleader. Update your morning alarm to pop up with a positive message like, 'Time to get up, gorgeous. You are doing great!'

c) Keep talking

One of the things that can affect our confidence the most is the false belief that we have nothing of note to say, or we are not worth listening to. This can happen in both our personal and professional lives and it is not helped when we feel like we are being shut down, people are speaking over us, or what we have to say is being blatantly ignored. It is easy to opt out and sit quiet, stop putting our hands up in order to offer our views and perspectives. This is especially the case when we are around pushy, dominant personalities that tend to butt in to what other people are saying, or simply speak more loudly so they cannot be ignored.

This is where you get to operate power instead of force. You won't need to fake arrogance or take on a false persona. The next time someone tries to interrupt you, keep talking. The next time someone starts to speak over you, keep talking. It might feel really awkward for the first few seconds and it's OK to expect to feel uncomfortable in this circumstance. However, the benefit of seeing through those few awkward seconds will be hugely rewarding in the short and the long run.

Don't worry about coming across as rude. It is the person who interrupted you that should learn to mind their manners. Pushy people often become pushy people because they are enabled. There are no boundaries or signals that their interrupting is not helpful or appreciated. By signalling to them that they can wait their turn, you will be extending more of a courtesy to them than they have for you, so don't feel bad about standing in your power, and keep talking.

Action tip: The next time you are having a conversation, finish your point and express yourself fully no matter who tries to interrupt you. Employ tact with your tone – you don't need to shout. You are innately powerful!

d) Keep more of your secrets

Secrets seem to get a bad rap and yet they are sacred containers we can use to grow and nurture ourselves and our dreams.

When you are working towards curing your comparison, space, time and silence around the moves you are making and the decisions you are taking are fundamental requirements. Too many times I have seen confidence destroyed by a well-meaning friend that although uninformed, offered an opinion they were not necessarily asked for.

If something is important to you then it is precious, unique and valuable. Do not let it become the fodder for an impromptu conversation or a source of gossip for other people who will have forgotten the exchange within ten minutes. You will be left with the aftermath of judgement to try and navigate and make sense of.

If you are thinking of leaving your job, pursuing a partner, getting a pet, asking someone to marry you, selling everything and travelling the world, trying to have a baby, trying not to have a baby, building a pond or setting up a community project . . . whatever it is, if it's important to you, BE QUIET.

Your uncle that runs a gardening business I'm sure is a very nice person but he's not the authority on starting the niche cookery blog you have been yearning to begin. Your partner might be a gifted linguist but no matter how well meaning, they cannot advise you on the investment plan you want to set up ASAP.

I'm not saying you have to push away those who care about you most, or close yourself off to important information and go it alone, and yet, be mindful and conscious about where you seek advice or guidance, as a word in the wrong direction can make your confidence leak all over the floor.

Before his passing, I saw the spiritual teacher and writer, Dr Wayne Dyer, speak onstage at an event in Glasgow. He passionately told us that when something is important to you, make a temple for it in your heart and guard it and this has really stuck with me through the years. Speaking to the 'wrong' person can be catastrophic for confidence, which might have taken months to build up and might only be in its early germination stages – it needs nurturing and protecting.

Ultimately, we protect our ideas and efforts by not being pulled into long discussions about them, so acknowledge the topic, be kind and yet shut the conversation down and move it on.

For example, when asked about the new business you have started: 'It's going well – we are working through some blocks, but thanks for asking. Are you going on holiday this year?'

Or when someone wants to stick their nose into your relationship: 'We are happy right now, so I don't have any news. Anyway, did I hear you have moved to a new house?'

You do not need to be cagey or make a big deal about it – just move the conversation along and shut down the interview-style interrogation that it has the potential to become. This keeps your secrets safe, your efforts supported and gives your confidence room to flourish.

Action tip: Prepare some of your own stock phrases that you can dish out and use in conversation as you navigate the liminal phases of your idea or belief's growth.

2. CONFIDENCE THROUGH YOUR APPROACH

a) Plan. Prepare. Perform.
Nothing wobbles confidence like poor planning. Many of us are so used to rushing around and multi-tasking that we struggle to prioritise our time and energy, and investment in our own goals always suffers.

Now fair enough, we all have that friend who seems to be unflappable no matter what is asked of them. They seem to be able to handle any challenge or opportunity, off the cuff, with ease. And then there are the rest of us who need a bit more time and space to be able to perform to our highest potential – it's a really unfair comparison to hold up those with rare, natural gifts as the norm!

I had a client who wanted to excel in her work and yet she would dread presentations or group meetings because she always felt like she had nothing of value to say and this was affecting how people perceived her contribution. Her boss was willing her on, but needed to see her leadership in action in order to put her forward for promotion – she was going to need to face this head on.

She realised that when it came to her unique working style she was in her element when she didn't feel rushed and had built-in pre-thinking and note-taking time, and yet she had built up a pattern of rushing from one meeting to the next with an ever-increasing feeling that she was chasing her tail.

We worked on an action plan so she would always be able to prepare ahead of time, to gather her relevant insights and share them thoughtfully whenever she was in the room. No meetings or presentations ever came out of the blue. She knew their purpose and who was attending – so she could anticipate and make plans ahead of time about how she could most positively contribute and make her presence known. She planned, was able to confidently prepare and then visibly perform, much to her and her manager's delight.

Action tip: Look at your schedule and work out which meetings or conversations provide an opportunity for you to shine and make a meaningful contribution. Make time to put in the work so you do not feel flustered or like you are winging it when meetings come around.

b) Stop borrowing drama from the future
How often do you find yourself thinking ahead, playing a disaster movie in your mind? It is so, so easy to borrow drama from the future – obsessing and over analysing all possible outcomes of a hypothetical situation in your imagination, all while the anxious feelings build and drain your energy and confidence. This feels even more acute when the comparison creep comes in and reminds you of how well other people seem to be doing and how they would never have ended up in the situation you think you will find yourself in.

We have to put a plug in this one. A golden way to stop this insidious habit is to dissolve worry by being radically present in the moment you are in right now. Give gratitude for what is on your plate, whether that is the people in your life, your dog at your feet, or simply your beating heart and breathing lungs that are keeping your system going. Worries keep us distracted and occupied with the things we cannot change, which means we lose our agency and leverage over the things we *can* change.

Action tip: The next time you start brewing up a disaster in your mind, catch yourself and immediately state three things that you are thankful for right now to root you firmly in the present.

C) Stay checked in
If a task or goal is sitting on my to-do list and I am avoiding it and pushing it around my plate, I know something is up. I always invite myself to check in on whether it is still important, relevant and resonant with who I am and where I want to see growth and change. I do this by journaling on the following prompts:

- Is this still important to me?

- Why?

- What, if any, are the benefits of continuing with this task/goal?

- What's my next right step?

Often this short exercise will get me fired up and reconnected with my own purpose and desires and I'll find new energy to get tasks done. This also works as a good nudge to crack on with those things that might have fallen out of focus but have been on the to-do list for a while. Or, if it is no longer aligned with my purpose, I let myself off the hook and prevent shame or guilt from accruing through my lack of action.

Often, it's what we choose not to do that can increase our self-confidence as it reinforces what we will do and focus on. If the journaling exercise above makes me feel a bit despondent or 'meh' then I take the task in question off the list and shelve the idea. This way I don't split my focus and I hold on to higher energy and motivation around what *is* important to me right now.

The payoff to this is I always have a sense of clarity and with this comes a boost in morale from knowing that I am on the right track and my inner critic or comparison creep can't invade my thoughts or upset my mood because I feel an ownership over my own life decisions.

Action tip: Make a list of the items and commitments that are currently occupying your time and focus. Check in on this to-do list and strike off the tasks that are not aligned with you in the present.

d) Practice non-attachment

Try not to tell yourself, 'I'll only get that good thing if certain conditions are met.' For many of us this will be a lifelong assignment that will come around like a boomerang and yet, when mastered this will bring a sense of calm, ease and trust to your life.

Non-attachment is a state of mind without clinginess, expectation, entitlement or dependence on a certain result. It is crucial to a good confidence supply as it brings about a consistent state of unflappability and can help you rise up to meet the challenging times in life with more resilience, and, when the good times are rolling, feel more presence and joy. It's important to not mistake non-attachment for detachment, however, as the two are very different. Detachment is being distant and disinterested, whereas the practice on which we focus here is:

- Not defining your happiness by anything outside of yourself

- Not having your dreams held ransom to circumstances outside your control

You know you are attached to a possession, aim, person or result when it feels like you won't be whole, complete, safe or successful if you don't have it or them. This is so closely linked with comparison because the emotions it brings about, such as anxiety, jealousy, envy and sadness, signal attachment. The fact is, we can't or won't always have what we desire in the way we want it. To believe that we will only be happy when we have ticked off all our goals, delays our happiness and outsources our power.

By practising non-attachment, we take back power and agency over our own happiness. With this comes stability, security and the confidence that no matter what happens we are going to be all right, as long as we stay true to ourselves.

Clues to how we are overly attached are all around us. It can be seen in thoughts such as:

- 'As long as I get that job offer I'll be as successful as that person . . .'

- 'If I can only make them want to date me then I too can find happiness . . .'

- 'If we can just go on holiday that will mean everything will work out . . .'

This isn't helped by the language of motivation being so fricking clingy and obsessive – 'never let go of your dream!', 'grab the bull by the horns!', 'crush your goals!', 'push, hustle, then push some more!,' etc.

When we approach anything like this we immediately constrict ourselves. There will always, always be another way and every different turn you were forced to make in your life to date provides the evidence for that! So, let's apply non-attachment to the examples above and note the sigh of relief and the space that comes with the new mindset:

- 'I feel so ready for that new career challenge and yet if I'm not selected I'll find another way . . .'

- 'I can't deny my attraction to them, and yet, if this doesn't turn into a second date I'm open to the next right person . . .'

- 'I would benefit from a break but if we can't go away I'm committed to giving this relationship the care and energy it needs for the highest good . . .'

Life and its experiences are not made to order and sent via Amazon Prime. So, no matter how convinced you are that your ideal outcome might look a certain way, take a particular length of time and have a list of predefined attributes, you could be wrong!

Action tip: Take a step back and look at where you are bringing force and entitlement to your words, decisions and actions. In doing so you are suffocating your efforts and ignoring other pathways and steps to get where you want to go. How can you reframe your beliefs?

3. CONFIDENCE THROUGH YOUR ACTIONS

a) Don't bring drama/negativity into what you are asking for

An important caveat – I am not advocating being nice for the sake of being nice as part of this. Well-placed anger is a necessary fuel to bring about change in the world we live in, which is so riddled with inequality. This is not your permission slip to ignore wrong-doing and just mask bad deeds with polite passivity or tone-police those people that are speaking up about their lived experience. Channelled anger is different to kicking up drama for the sake of it, and we both know it.

Mastering how to communicate powerfully can work wonders for our confidence, especially when it comes to our delivery, which is often as important as our words. A situation or conversation will be influenced by the way you come at it – specifically, your energy, tone and intention, so make sure you keep each of these in check. What you put out there, you will get back directly or indirectly – don't let it be an 'ouch!'.

This means that if you are bringing drama, entitlement or a bad attitude to a situation then you can expect the results of your efforts to be tinged by those. And yet if you bring calm power, the benefit of the doubt and confidence you will almost always meet what you want halfway, diffusing even the most heated of tensions.

When we are choosing not to participate in drama or panic, our confidence can softly purr and help us show up fully and act in a way that is laden with integrity, authenticity and also maturity. Put into action, this means not sending multi-paragraph, emotive emails when you're angry and you feel you have been let down. Give yourself a couple of hours and let the calm and capable you lead those talks.

It means apologising when you are in the wrong and letting your new behaviour show that you mean it. 'I'm sorry' doesn't mean anything if it's followed quickly by 'but'. You're either sorry or you're not.

Rather than throwing yourself into a monologue on the shop floor explaining your reasons why the top isn't quite right, it's just asking for a refund. Maya at the till just wants to get the line down and go on her lunch break – stick to the critical info! Ultimately, the fluff, huff, puff and fuss that surrounds so many of our interactions are often unhelpful and dissolve away our confidence rather than supporting it. We end up coming over as unnecessarily apologetic.

....

Action tip: Be honest – where are you bringing a bit of drama and making things a big deal when they could be dealt with smoothly and swiftly? How can you switch up how you are acting?

....

b) Keep an evidence journal so you know all the good things you've done

Our brains are absolutely brilliant at picking out and remembering our faults, trip ups and shortcomings. So much so that we often brush aside and even ignore altogether the signs we are getting every single day that things are playing out positively.

So that I can stay aware and motivated for the rest of the week, before bed every night I'll write down the things in my day that went well and collect the evidence that I am experiencing the growth, change and progress that is most important to me.

This can be a real mix of a list including:

- Was running late for my meeting but she was even later so I looked on time – woo!

- Got a reply from that brand I love – they are interested!

- My IG post today was really well received – what a relief

- My client loved the ideas board I helped them with. We are running ahead of schedule – this is so great for both of us

- Etc., etc.

Some of the 'evidence' that feels noteworthy will be a direct response to my own efforts and other positive occurrences will be down to synchronicity or a lucky break. It doesn't matter though – they all go down in my evidence journal and when I'm having a tough day and my confidence is low, I go straight back to those pages to remind myself that the life I want is unfolding for me.

Action tip: Invest in a new notebook and pen to keep next to your bed. Every day collect down the positive things that have happened and read back over your notes every couple of weeks for that extra confidence boost.

c) Break down your goal – little steps are easier to achieve

Confidence can't grow if you are constantly being overwhelmed. Use your self-focus as a tool to laser in on the composite parts of the wider goal you are working towards and break these down into chunks. This will promote clarity around the action to take and help you leverage your situation and resources.

So, for example, if your goal is to leave your current job by August, picture that end result and work backwards – how can you break that down into several steps?

It might include reviewing your current CV and understanding the updates needed, then making the updates. Next, it might be refreshing your LinkedIn and making new connections in the company or area you would like to join. Next comes your outreach emails and phone calls and so on.

Each of these actions builds on the one before and allows you to show up for your bigger goal without being overwhelmed with the size of the task. We often underestimate what we can do in a few years but overestimate what we can do in one year, so be kind to yourself on the timing of the steps you decide. It's better to reach your goal and tick off that achievement even if there is a twisting, turning timeline, rather than not achieve it at all because it felt like too much of a hill to climb.

Action tip: Thinking about the goals you set in Chapter 3, what can you do to break these down and make them even more bitesize?

d) Back yourself and do the thing

How many times have you shot down one of your own ideas or not taken action on something because you, and you alone, have decided it wouldn't work out? We have decided not to back ourselves and instead rejected ourselves and squashed our own value.

This shows up in various ways, like not even applying for a job because you think you won't get it (says who?), not putting yourself forward to write for someone's blog because you don't think you are good enough (on what evidence?), dropping your love of playing music as if it hasn't taken off now then it never will (totally true if you stop!).

Harvesting little bits of courage and using these to power micro actions is rocket fuel for growing confidence. And all it takes is you letting your ideas get off the drawing board and believing in the possibility they might come off, just a micro amount – not even a lot!

Action tip: Start to doubt your doubt and instead replace it with an attitude of 'what if?'. Take action and do the thing that you might ordinarily have rejected as an option. Write the blog, text that person the question, apply for the position – do the thing!

Recap on your keys to confidence

There are a wealth of options in this chapter for you to try in order to grow your self-confidence. Not all of these will be relevant to you – it could well be you are already operating strongly in a few areas, which I hope is the case.

So that you can put some time into those areas that might need a bit more work, consider the recap exercise below and draft how you can put these keys to confidence to work in your life, including the Action Tip!

Confidence through your words	How can you implement the advice tip in your life?
Speak your truth	
Personal pep talks	
Keep talking	
Keep more secrets	

Confidence through your approach	How can you implement the advice tip in your life?
Plan. Prepare. Perform.	
Stop borrowing drama from the future	
Decide it's not important	
Practice non-attachment	

Confidence through your actions	How can you implement the advice tip in your life?
Don't make it a big deal	
Keep an evidence journal	
Break it down. Then break it down again.	
Back yourself and do the thing	

The above confidence keys can be used daily to help support the work you have already completed relating to your own sense of focus.

However you might describe the state of your confidence at this moment, wherever you are now, staying committed to working your confidence muscles will deliver huge rewards for you and your goals.

By arriving at your own working definition of confidence and its characteristics, you can focus more on that rather than the behaviour of other people.

Equally, I invite you to stay aware of how you can use your words, your approach and your deeds to power up your confidence and try and keep your inner fire burning so you can show up and work diligently towards what you want most.

CHAPTER 6

BUILDING THE RIGHT ENVIRONMENT

'What you feed your mind, will lead your life'
Kemi Sogunle

In the previous chapter we focused much of our energy on what you can be doing as an individual to make tweaks in your outlook and behaviour as part of curing comparison. This next step, however, will be centred on looking at the world around us, and dispelling some of the myths about what it is to 'make it'. A big part of this involves you taking back your power and exercising your discernment and choice to create conditions – the right environment – for your 'you-ness' to thrive.

Get ready to let go of the success checklist, dissolve your tendency to look at what others are doing and consciously curate the influences in your life for your ultimate reward.

Building an abundant mindset – there's enough for each of us

Comparing tricks us into thinking we are missing out. We have all been there. It is a Sunday morning, we are scrolling in our PJ's and suddenly we see that a friend has posted about an achievement that we have been yearning for or working towards ourselves. Perhaps it's a new job at a famous tech company, they have smashed a wellness goal, or it could be a new sparkler on the ring finger.

On seeing the news come through, rather than warm feelings of congratulations, something more sinister lurks in our emotional reaction . . . 'Oh, FFS . . . they don't deserve it. What about me? When will it be my turn? Be happy for them? You must be joking! They took my chance!'

Ah, the bitter taste of losing out that the 'zero-sum game' presents. That is, the belief that a win for someone else means one less chance for you or, even worse, no chance at all because of their gain or progress. It is almost as if jobs, lovers, babies, travel and awards are finite in supply and seeing your comparison trigger take away from the supply makes it harder for you to achieve the same happiness in your own way. This makes zero sense, but when did that ever stop us comparing?

Rationally, we should view someone else's win as inspiration to keep going and stay committed to reaching that achievement ourselves as there in plain sight is the proof that it can be done! But the comparison trap you have fallen into won't let you go there. It is scary how comparison twists our perception, and rather than seeing someone else's success as evidence of what is possible, we use it as a stick to beat ourselves. This also inserts a wedge between us and that other person.

My DMs overflow with messages from people suffering with this exact scenario, so if you feel it too you are not alone. 'I know how hard she worked for that job, but I wanted it too . . .' 'I love my friend, but he has it so easy when it comes to dating and I resent him for it . . .' 'I support her work, but I have been doing this longer and it is not fair she has such a big social-media following . . .'

It is all too easy for our thoughts to stay in this place of lack, scarcity, distance and comparison. It is so familiar to so many of us and the emotional pain is like a warm bath; that is, it's easier to stay where we are and wallow than climb out and go for the growth we know will lead us to where we want to be. It's a bit like an uncomfortable comfort zone.

This is why it is so crucial to ensure we are creating mindsets that provide a welcome and nurturing environment for what we want to achieve, which starts with what goes on between our ears.

Start feeding the good wolf

When it comes to achievement and success, we need to flip our perspective so that rather than being stuck in the mindset of scarcity, we can tune in to the frequency of possibility and abundance. Just like you can search for a radio channel and listen to different music and DJs, you can change the soundtrack in your head and in doing so change the environment of your thoughts. Play a more positive daily soundtrack and pivot through the hot jealous moments, coming out the other side, to a place of self-focus and self-motivation. It is dangerous to underestimate the importance of our thoughts and what we believe about ourselves as this so strongly influences our reality.

'Two Wolves' is a story I often share in my client workshops that illustrates the complexity and balance of our negative and positive thoughts with goose-pimple-inducing effect. It is also one I revisit myself when I find the self-critical thoughts becoming overwhelming. To paraphrase, the adage goes:

A grandfather is talking to his grandson about life and shares how he feels, explaining the conflict going on inside him. It involves two wolves – one is evil and represents anger, envy, sorrow, regret, greed and arrogance and so on. The second wolf represents the good qualities he has within him, like joy, peace, love, hope, humility and kindness. The grandfather next says that all people experience the same internal fight and the wee boy asks, 'Which one will win?' To which the elder responds, 'The one you feed.'

Which one do you tend to feed most regularly?

Comparison falls under the evil wolf's remit and, in order to nourish and feed our own good wolf, awareness is key. We can make the switch through some fundamental reframing, take these as examples:

- Your friend opens her own Etsy store even though you have been talking about doing it for ages – time to get your art online!

- Your sibling reaches a wellness goal – your own health path is waiting for you!

- You hear another happy story of finding love later in life and getting pregnant quickly – there is life outside disappointing Tinder dates!

- Your ex-colleague quits their job and goes travelling around the world – dust off your passport and sit down and make a savings plan!

Ultimately, thinking back to the story, what can you do, say or be to feed your good wolf and keep comparison at bay?

I am committed to being a lifelong learner when it comes to this area and I always have my eyes and ears open for ways I can feed my good wolf and keep comparison at bay. I picked up this next remedy from my friend and fellow coach Corinne Worsley and when she shared it, I snaffled it away like a truffle pig (how's that for a visual?).

To further provide a harmonious environment for your own dreams to thrive, she told me when you see someone showing signs of living their life in a certain way, and it triggers your 'what about me?!' tendency, you can also activate this powerful affirmation:

'Good for you! And the same for me!'[17]

Let me break it down. This works because you simply cannot be in comparison envy and rooting for yourself in the same moment, so your brain will override the negative judgement with the positivity firehose that is this statement.

When you state the affirmation, you are able to reset your thoughts and with this, get back in your own lane rather than letting comparison take hold and whisking you down a rabbit hole of negative thinking.

....

Action tip: To increase its potency, say the words out loud and point your finger at the screen/person and then at yourself to really feel the belief take root in your body. 'Good for you! And the same for me!'

Ultimately, someone else getting what they want, whether you believe they deserve it or not, does not mean a failure for you. Arguably it does not mean anything. It is information that can choose to serve the fire in your belly or burn and destroy your potential. Choose wisely.

....

Reflect on the things that have triggered your comparison recently. Be honest about when and how these came about and journal here what you saw that brought on a comparison attack . . .

....

....

....

....

....

....

How does it feel to know you can swap your judgement for inspiration?

....

....

....

....

....

....

....

These two tools will serve you well as we move on because the perceived timing of individual progress is one of the biggest comparisons triggers out there.

Don't be constrained by milestones and timing

At any one time we will each have a view on whether we are ahead, behind or on par with the pace of the people we compare ourselves to, or perhaps how we are progressing towards a certain milestone. Sometimes this can be a great motivation and help you work out the connecting steps to propel you forward. In my own life I have assessed how I was doing with judgements like, 'OK, well, Sarah got to that position when she was twenty-eight so I'll have a certain job title by <insert number>', 'My mum and dad met at twenty-six so I'll find a partner by <insert number>', 'Abdul has just bought a home at thirty-eight so I will buy a house by <insert number>', 'That blogger got to 50k in three years so I will have this amount of social media followers by <insert number>'.

We can become obsessive about timing and how long it takes to hit the milestones that we perceive to matter. With this in mind, is there anything more infuriating and exasperating than to notice someone seemingly, out of nowhere, swoop in and precociously scoop up the prize you have been working towards or held dear for so long, leaving your timings in the dirt?

I experienced this recently when I saw a blogger who is much younger than me announce he had been chosen to do a second TEDx Talk – something that has been on my wish list since I started out in the self-development industry. I have followed and respected the likes of Brené Brown and the novelist Chimamanda Ngozi Adichie for years thanks to watching their TED Talks, and to see someone who I judged to be uninitiated, undeserving and less experienced than me take the stage prematurely, made my blood boil, I am embarrassed to admit.

This was a big wakeup call and living with the knowledge of their accomplishment felt like walking around with a stone in my shoe as I forensically stalked their social media to try to uncover how he had done it.

> **If you are really honest with yourself, who specifically have you judged to be less deserving, experienced or capable than you?**

We have been hypnotised by the myth of overnight success, which is so at odds with creating an abundant environment in which our own dreams can flourish. The truth is, it takes a long time to be an instant hit and nobody gets to skip the work, no matter what a nonchalant social-media post might suggest to the contrary.

We will never truly know the work – emotional, physical, practical and spiritual – that goes into someone else's toil that then produces an end result. Nothing happens overnight. There are endless examples to help us understand the reality of the time, money, effort and faith that your version of success will expect you to invest – we already touched on some before, but who am I to limit the inspiration?

J.K. Rowling used rock bottom as her solid foundation and nourished a creative idea that just would not go away. That big idea was *Harry Potter and the Philosopher's Stone*, and we all know the end of that story! Yet the lead up to her being picked up by a publishing house at age 31 was tumultuous to say the least, and includes the death of a parent, taking up a teaching job abroad and entering and exiting her marriage. It was only when she was back in Britain, a penniless single mother, that she summoned all the determination needed to finish the original draft of her book that became such an iconic success.

Having combated depression herself, Lilly Singh, the Canada-based comedian, started a YouTube channel in 2010 to help others. Fast-forward to today and over 14 million subscribers later, and Singh is reportedly one of the most successful women on YouTube. She's created videos with the likes of Michelle Obama and Dwayne Johnson, has a world tour under her belt and is on her way to becoming one of the biggest social-media voices of a generation.

Can you imagine if creatives like this had not kept at it? Or been deterred into quitting because they felt inferior to their peers?

Motivation success stories

It is not just these well-known names that reveal what the path to success can look like. You will find examples relevant to you much closer to home too, and seeking these out is a brilliant way to ramp up your own motivation and belief in your own path. That cousin of yours who has paid off all their debt – take them for a beer/coffee/whatever and find out what it took. Your friend who has tripled their Instagram following in only a few months – ask them to share their approach or perspective.

Your uncle who has thrived running his own business – reach out and ask to hear his story.

You can guarantee that your own path will be different and yet soaking up their story can add to your inspiration bank. Collecting evidence and data in an area of success you are seeking for yourself will put you squarely in your own lane as you realise with clarity that we each have an individually assigned path to walk. This, in addition, will help you trust the timing of your own life and keep the faith that it can and WILL happen for you. Success is never linear and to plot against only age or time taken, rather than growth, massively devalues the journey to get where we want to go.

It is impossible to be 'ahead' or 'behind' as life just does not work like that – your time zone is your time zone, just like New York has a

different time zone to Barcelona. The more we can apply this interpretation to both our personal and work lives, the better off we will
be and the more conducive our minds will be to positive progress.

**The next time you get caught up on the timing of
things happening for you, or observe the mirage of an
overnight success, reflect on these points:**

- **What is happening in your time zone right now?**

....
....

- **Where would you like to slow down?**

....
....

- **Where would you like to speed up?**

....
....

- **What is the next right step you can take to bring
  about the shift you would like to achieve?**

....
....

- **Who can you reach out to in order to gather data
  and information about getting to where you want to
  be?**

....
....

Your answers to these questions, written in your journal or on your smart phone notes app, will snap you back into your present and peel away comparison's claws. This is so key to creating an environment where you and your own vision for your life – instead of comparison – can thrive.

Burn the arbitrary checklist

Something that worries me is seeing the markers of success and milestones in life boiling down to an arbitrary checklist of social-media status updates. Relationship? Check. House purchased? Check. Couple of holidays a year? Check. Children? Check. Great job? Check. Nice car (with the monthly lease fee to match)? Check.

For many people these experiences can form the foundations of a full, vibrant life where we put a roof over the heads of those we love and get to travel and enjoy the sights of the world with a cherished partner by our side as we strive to better ourselves and make a difference in some way. If this is you, then all power to you – there is a lot to be said in support of all of the above.

And yet, how many of these choices are influenced by a feeling we are supposed to seek and pass these milestones? Do you ever stop to reflect along the way as to what is driving you in a certain direction – is it your own will and vision, or society's?

Thinking about your own life, have you inherited from your past a pressure to 'keep up' in some way?

To what extent have you been driven by what you feel you should be doing? Perhaps score yourself from one to ten (one being not at all, ten being very much so!).

Recall where this voice or pressure came from, e.g. a vocal parent, hearing friends discuss their lives, criticism from a colleague . . .

So many of our behaviours, choices and decisions originate from a place of 'should', and with this comes compromise as when we are driven by 'should' we cannot be led by 'I desire', 'I want', 'I am motivated by', 'I choose', 'I can make a difference'. It removes your personal drive, your authority and your responsibility from your individual success equation and this allows comparison to thrive.

Comparison and regret

As you continue to create the right environment to cure comparison, I want you to change tack a bit. This next section will see us focus in on your relationship with yourself and acknowledging some of the experiences that may not have been easy to work through. Our aim is to reduce the space they take up in our thoughts, and to do this we need to look at making peace with our past.

> *'To forgive is to set a prisoner free and discover the*
> *prisoner was you'*
> – Lewis B. Smedes

Do you ever find yourself revisiting painful scenarios or experiences from your past? When the past feels like a heavy load, we can find ourselves:

- Comparing our life now to what it could have been had we made a different choice or taken a chance ('If only I had not married her', or 'If only I'd gone travelling instead!', etc.)

- Comparing how we are doing in relation to those who have experienced the same thing, and feeling inferior because they seem free and healed ('How come they seem to be OK with going bankrupt and I live in fear of being found out?')

- Comparing how we rank in relation to people who have not experienced the same thing and feeling resentment that they have it easy ('It will never happen for me – their parents were not messed up like mine were, so it was always going to be easier for them').

To overcome these difficult reflections, we must start to let go of the blocks and barriers that are holding us back and make peace with ourselves too, and in doing so allow for healing and growth to replace the shame and regret.

Even the thought of 'going there' with our more personal, sensitive experiences can bring up so much resistance for us. It feels like a heavy topic that scratches at our fragility and vulnerability, but I want you to know it is safe for you to explore this in your own way, at your own pace. If your journey continues on to take you to special support in the shape of therapy and groups, then all power to you.

Making peace with past experiences

The benefits of making peace with your past are many and include:

- It is an act of kindness to yourself – it is a gift you give yourself.

- There doesn't need to be any reconciliation or confrontation – you don't even have to be in the same room as the person who wronged you.

- You do not need that apology that is never coming anyway.

- It does not mean you have to stop feeling – you don't need to suppress or ignore your emotions or the pain you feel about a situation.

- It does not equate to forgetting, it does not rewrite history – but it will help you rewrite your story.

Although no single technique is proven, and what follows does not replace or usurp professional support and therapy, the steps below can work to release the past and help you be really, truly and fully yourself today.

> **Write down here the things, people, conversations, emotional baggage and experiences that you want to release and make peace with, and get on with your life.**

Now let's look at the ways you can move forward, having acknowledged these.

1. LET IT OUT

When we acknowledge the hurt and we are honest with ourselves we can come to accept what happened, which leaves room for the healing. To do this, you might want to write it down, capture it in a song, poem or piece of art or find a therapist who can help you express what happened. Choose what feels right for you and will allow the release, and if it takes a few attempts to get the feelings out, do not judge yourself harshly. You might have been blocking these feelings for years and dissolving these barriers may not happen overnight. You need and deserve to fully express how the wrongdoing made you feel.

....

Action tip: Write a letter to your past self and note down all the ways you have grown since that period of time. Positively praise the person you were then and shower them with the love and kindness you would give to a best friend, had they had the same experience.

....

2. STEP INTO YOUR PROTECTION BUBBLE

Feeling safe and secure means we can be our own best friend and make confident choices that will support us in the life we want to lead, free from comparison.

To do this, imagine yourself in a sphere of space where nothing can touch you – a bit like a zorb. Doing this activates a feeling of an invisible force-field around you, placing you firmly in the present. I tend to choose a golden bubble of light that I see surrounding me whenever I need to feel protected and put the world at arm's length. Ideally, if you can, find a quiet place in which to do this – although you can certainly do it in anywhere; I sometimes do this on busy public transport. Close your eyes and imagine yourself in a golden bubble with about a metre of space all around you in each direction, breathe deeply, filling your body with life-giving oxygen and feel the sensation of calm wash over you and restore a positive mood.

From the state that this technique creates, we can then put in place other ways to make ourselves feel secure in our present.

Action tip: Set a reminder on your phone or online diary each morning to activate your bubble of protection and imagine it surrounding you. Top up with an extra layer before a tricky liaison, like meeting an ex or having to present to your tyrant of a boss – I rarely go anywhere without putting myself in my 'Lucy Zorb'. Tag me on social media if you need an accountability buddy.

3. ACKNOWLEDGE THE VALUES THAT YOU LIVE BY TODAY

The reason we become hung up on the past and store its emotional baggage is often because what we might have done before is not congruent with how we choose to live today, or what we might do if we were given our time again.

By identifying our present standards and values, we can achieve clarity as to 'why' we are in pain over what we did or did not do.

Action tip: Go back to your list of values that you defined for yourself in Chapter 3 and make sure you keep them somewhere you can see or access regularly. Read them when you get up in the morning and before you go to bed at night so you can be present with what is important to you.

4. REMEMBER YOU ARE ONLY HUMAN

So much clarity comes from reflecting with hindsight. If you learn from it, the situation was not wasted, and you will avoid repeating the behaviour.

When you learned how to swim, there was probably a fair bit of splashing around and drinking more pool water than you would have liked before you got the hang of it and confidently found your stride – we expected it to take a while to get the hang of. And if you are yet to learn how to swim, the chances are you know this will be part of your experience at the beginning too, when you take a dip.

It's the same with new ways of being and developing new thinking patterns – these are skills that take time to integrate. For this reason, give yourself a break while you adopt these new ways of being and commit to doing better and learning from your past experiences.

....

Action tip: When you notice those thoughts of the past cropping up and tormenting you, use the affirmation, 'Every day and in every way, I am doing my best to grow'.

These tools ground us firmly in the present and keep us aware of the mindset changes we can use to build the right environment in which to thrive. Through doing this we can become even clearer about how we can truly be ourselves, because of, or in spite of, the turns our life might have taken.

And speaking of being ourselves, this next step will build on this further and see any habits of 'pretending' unravel – let's check in on where we might be mimicking others, consciously or otherwise.

....

Drop the tribute act

When we are young – I mean really little – imitating others signals a big jump in our development.

Mimicking the sound of a family member's voice, waving back at people waving at us as we sit in the supermarket trolley, trying not to fall over as we try to wear our big brother's shoes around the house or copying the dance moves of our classmate at the local kids' disco are all natural types of mimicry that help us learn how the world works and, crucially, understand ourselves. We learn our way of doing things and develop our own mannerisms and behaviours totally unique to ourselves and our personality.

As we grow older, however, the ability to mimic can take a sinister turn. We use the inspiration of others in a way that means we start to lean on, model and copy the behaviour, traits, style and moves of others because we feel like to be accepted or be successful, we have to be more like them. I call this the 'tribute act trap'. Sometimes called a covers band, a tribute act is a performer or group that plays the songs of, and has the same look of, a famous pop act and will often have a quirky, tongue-in-cheek name.

So, if you can't book actual Elton John for your birthday party (surprise!), you might instead see 'Elton Wrong'. I remember seeing Bjorn Again – an ABBA tribute band – support the Spice Girls and they were absolutely amazing. I digress – the point is that ultimately a tribute act is a dressing up, an imitation.

When we are in the tribute act trap, we get caught up in the tendency to borrow from and emulate the look of someone else's life because our comparison voice says, 'Be like them,' rather than, 'What's my way to achieve something similar and be myself?' We are trying to pass off and adopt their attributes and behaviours as our own.

To give some examples, in the past, I have had clients identify their own tribute-act tendencies to be:

- Shopping at the same place as their comparison trigger – even though it put her under financial pressure – because she wanted to mimic their style, rather than get creative and find her own sartorial interpretation

- Listening to the same music as their comparison trigger because they thought it would make them 'cooler', rather than letting their own ears decide

- Enrolling in a training course in a far off land because their comparison avatar had and she thought, therefore, it was the only route to get where she wanted (it wasn't)

You can try and be like something but can never actually be it. Just like a musical tribute act versus the real McCoy – it will only ever be an imitation. It can never pass for the real thing. And why would you want it to pass? We should be looking to express ourselves and only ourselves.

Which is why we should be open to the tips, hints and methods that help us get real on who we are and where we are going. Sure, we can act on inspiration – it is all around us – but let's not get caught up in trying to shoehorn ourselves into the shoes of others.

....

Action tip: Rather than just mindlessly copying someone, look at their journey and experiences and, with distance and objectivity, ask yourself, 'How does this translate to me and my life today? How can this example help me be more authentic and true to my own dreams?'

....

How to be inspired by other people rather than imitating them

It is possible to study those people that provide oodles of inspiration and illustrate the possibility of achieving what appeals most to you. This only works if we engage our 'find the crystal' approach we were first introduced to in Chapters 1 and 3 and we stay open and committed to gleaning the information that serves our own dreams and goals. This is a research exercise: complete it swiftly, efficiently, and then get out of there!

Turning inspiration into our own knowledge borrows from a neuro-linguistic programming technique called modelling. The ways my clients and I have done this in the past is modelling from afar, which includes techniques like:

- Find interviews, features, blog posts, Netflix documentaries and biographical films of people you admire and take some notes on what strikes you as the key steps they took or turning points they experienced. You might even sketch out timelines, detailing which steps came first, the support this person had, the mistakes they made, their daily routine, how they honed their skills, etc. This does not mean you have to copy or be guided by their timings, and yet it can provide an idea of the potential for what to expect.

- Find the people in real life that inspire you and follow them, or their cohort, on social media and watch their videos to pick up on the energy, pace and day-to-day happenings of their lives to get a front-row seat to the progress in progress. You will see other people doing things in their own way, which gives you permission to do the same.

- Notice and acknowledge the results and attributes that you seek, and that are aligned with your own results. For example, share enthusiastic congratulations with that person who has won the award that you hope to one day hold. If someone says something funny and their intoxicating charm lights up the room, tell them that they made your night! It might feel tough at first, but it is so much better than harbouring resentment and follows the ethos of 'good for you and the same for me!' that we learned earlier.

To reiterate, these steps are not intended to give you permission to compare yourself (as if!) but rather they're an invitation to take a step back and realise that there are so many ways you can achieve the goals you are pursuing. At this stage, if this feels like too much to ask of yourself, revisit this section when you have completed the rest of the book – it will feel much easier. After all, your version of success is leaving you clues, and it is up to each of us to ensure our environment is not a hostile one.

Creating conditions for you to bloom

'When a flower doesn't bloom, you fix the environment in which it grows, not the flower'
– Alexander Den Heijer

To arrive at this point in our literary journey together you will have undertaken some significant, challenging and, I hope, rewarding inner work. You now have a clear vision, or an emerging one, of what your life could hold for you and what your next action steps might be.

As much as I'm a big advocate for taking responsibility for what we experience in our lives, it is impossible to ignore that routines, relationships and our environment do have an effect on us too. Ultimately, curing your comparison depends on this next tranche of work we will complete together as we will be diving deep into your current environment.

To build on the flower quote above, you need space, good soil for your roots and perfectly placed support in order to grow strongly from the ground up.

Just like any growth, this part of the process can be testing and stretching. It's also going to ask you to put yourself front and centre in your life today and renegotiate and reprioritise accordingly, which is not something that comes easily to many of us.

This doesn't need to be traumatic

Some of the outputs of this next period of reflection might see you end ties with or distance yourself from people you have known for a long time. Conversely, it might also prompt you to reach out to strangers that you feel called to contact.

You will be asked to make some select decisions that may be uncomfortable, and yet, at the same time, these do NOT have to be traumatic, confrontational or distressing to you or other parties. (Although you would be forgiven for believing the opposite.)

Simply selecting who has our time and attention might feel like it needs to come with a declaration, monologue or supporting state-ment in the shape of a multi-paragraphed post on social media. Well, I am here to tell you it doesn't – not even close.

On any given day, on opening an app, I will see a post exclaiming how someone has *'done a much-needed friends cull, so if you can see this, you have made the cut!'* On another app: *'I'm unfollowing loads of people at the moment.'* And in real-life, the burn-and-destroy approach seems to prevail too: *'I cut them out of my life after that,'* whatever 'that' may be.

The thing is, you can create a space in your current relationships and even end a friendship in a drama-free way, and nobody has to know, it doesn't need to be made into a big public scene. So, breathe that deep exhale and enjoy that sigh of relief that comes from knowing you can make the decisions you need to without holding any press conferences as a result.

In these next chapters, we will be looking at both the online and offline worlds to ensure you are creating the social and familial conditions in which to thrive, making space for support, collabora-tion and community. Why? Because to recall the quote above that highlights the flower, we must ensure you are surrounded with what it takes for you to bloom, that your emotional needs are nourished and your belief in yourself is watered.

Different types of toxic friends

Something that never fails to surprise me is how good we are at ignoring or enabling the poor behaviour of others, even when these have serious sabotaging effects on our life:

- 'Oh, she doesn't really mean it when she body-shames me – it's just a bit of banter'

- 'They are trying to protect me – that's why they are so opinionated about my career'

- 'I have known them since school so they have always "kept it real" with me'

And yet deep down we know the comments we receive, in the tone they are delivered, are not just a bit of banter or 'real talk'. Actually the truth is that perhaps your sibling would like you to look differently and does not accept you as you are. Perhaps rather than knowing best, your partner does not want you to shine brighter in your work because of their own insecurities and, in reality, your old group of friends just don't get you and do not take you seriously. We can become immune to the snipes and little digs of the people in our social and family circles as we let their insecurities be a louder voice and stronger force than our own trusted TYG (True You Guide).

All too often their insidious interference and influence keeps us stuck to the spot and too afraid to be ourselves, and this creates the perfect conditions for comparison to thrive. We observe other people making moves in their lives, and yet all we feel we can do is stare, aware we don't have the backing of those around us, and without it, we feel weak and worthless.

Ouch, right?

'The truth will set you free. But first, it will piss you off'
– Gloria Steinem

Just like ripping off a Band-Aid, this next bit might hurt, so we are going to deal with it quickly and effectively: some of the people closest to you might not be rooting for you to do well, to grow and to thrive. Pay attention to those that might not clap when you win, even though acknowledging this toxicity can feel really confronting.

However, caring enough about your future to seek out the individuals and communities that will reward you with warmth and reciprocity requires you to love yourself enough to say no to toxic energies. No matter how longstanding their presence may be in your life.

Before you put those judgemental pants on and start believing this next exercise is about 'draining the swamp' or other hyperbole, let us remember it's not simply a case of 'them' (the toxic people – the baddies) and 'us ' (being the clean-as-a-whistle goodies).

Cleaning up your energy field only works if you bring with you all the compassion and humility you can possibly summon. We have been in their shoes too! Let us remember, as hard as it is to stomach, we each have made mistakes and manipulated others to serve our own needs and wants. We have cheated, lied, fibbed and acted in ways that now make us cringe. It is the changing of our own behaviour, staying aware of our intentions, taking the lessons and moving on in which the acts of atonement are contained.

Toxic people and toxic behaviours are all around us and yet, rather than attach blame and dwell there, let's focus on spotting them and getting the hell out of there. You will perhaps have extra personas to add to this list, which is not intended to be exhaustive, but let's start by reviewing these common and repeat offenders:

The 'prove it' person. They will regularly make you feel you have to choose between them and something or someone else, e.g., 'If you loved me you would spend the whole weekend with me instead of seeing your friends,' or 'If you were really my friend you would be coming to yoga with me later.' And let's be clear, there never ever seems to be enough proof for them to feel satisfied, does there? They continue to demonstrate that they need more and better gestures and words from you in order to make them happy.

Can't handle your joy. These ones just can't seem to get on board with your good news and will find a way to try and 'bring you back down to earth'. They are individuals who, when things are going well, say things like 'Yeah it's all very well you are going on holiday, but think of all the work that will have piled up when you get home!' Conversely, if there is bad news, they are happy to wallow, bitch and moan with you about it, and stay with you in a slump.

The knife-twisters. Through their words and hints they will make their opinions and analysis of you and your own thoughts and actions clear. And if you make a mistake, they won't let you forget it! You might confess, 'I really wish I hadn't sent that email' and rather than trying to support you and help you feel better, they will be straight in with, 'Yeah, the timing was off but more than that it got shared around, didn't it? So, the worst is yet to come!' It's like they love to prod the bruise or twist the knife.

The 'me, me, me'. This one will be well known to you if you recognise when you are around them you hardly say a word. Why would you be so quiet? They are often delivering monologues to you about their lives, or latest drama, and there are never any questions coming your way. They are interested only in themselves and it simply isn't a two-way street.

The black hole. They want to always be in control of everything and everyone around them. These relationships can feel a bit like being sucked into a black hole because when you are around them, you disappear for periods of time. They might tell you how to dress, where to be, what to say. If you disagree, they will so fervently argue their point that eventually they wear you down. They want you to be like them and think like them and they are perhaps the most dangerous toxic people of them all. Especially in positions of power, like your boss, your partner or parent.

There are more avatars of toxicity and yet the ones featured here are some of the main offenders that occupy our social and family circles. If you are really unlucky, a variety of these characters might currently be present in your life. Although it may not be possible to eradicate toxic people from our lives overnight, it is possible, and necessary, to remove them from the main positions of influence in it.

Looking at who is 'round your table'

The psychological writer Jim Rohn notably highlighted: 'You are the average of the five people you spend the most time with.'[18]

Do the people you see and speak to the majority of the time bring you what you need? If there were six seats around a table, one chair for you and five chairs surrounding it, who would currently be seated with you? Family, friends, co-workers, people you are connected with on social media . . . if you were to complete a quick audit now, who currently has a seat?

Write down the names of five people who would sit at your table:

1. ....

2. ....

3. ....

4. ....

5. ....

And based on this, what spontaneous thoughts come up for you? Negative or positive, please pay attention as this is unique inner guidance.

Are you happy and hopeful at the potential of what the average of those people is? In other words, do you feel you have in place the people that will be key to you achieving your own version of success?

Or are you worried and concerned by what that might mean for you right now? In that the people who you spend the most time with are absolutely not facilitators of your own happiness.

How conscious or unconscious has this decision
been? Are you realising that some friendships have
stayed with you because of habit rather than genuine
connection?

Calling to mind your future self and the aspirations
you have right now, to what extent are these aligned
with the people that surround you? For example, can
you see you growing together as a cohort?

How supportive are they of you and your growth?
That does not mean they are deferential and won't
challenge you!

Often this exercise gives people the heebie-jeebies – technical term – as it highlights where our social and family circles fall short when it comes to having our needs met. But once we have identified where the problems lie, we can do something about them.

Curating your seats so your environment thrives

Nobody at your table should inherit a seat, be there by accident or simply have a place because of the time you have known each other or because they are popular with others.

This even applies to blood ties and family – just because you are related to someone does not mean they automatically have to be around the table. You can still love them hard and see them often but when it comes to the table, they may be sat somewhere different for a while. This especially applies to you if there are members of your family that, although they may be well meaning, can bring you down.

Those closest to you shape your success, your interests and your experience, so this really matters, and it must be a meritocratic process to secure a chair. Assessing the value, benefit and love that people add or remove from your life allows us to attract those to us that have the same high standards and cycle of growth.

The betterment of ourselves and those around us continues and perpetuates and the significance of this should not be underestimated. The conscious decisions you start to make in this area are worth your time as:

Your intellect needs to be stimulated and your beliefs challenged so that you can be an empathetic and productive human, working the muscles of both your brain and your heart. Nobody benefits from having narrow perspectives or existing in an echo chamber of opinions – our circle should stretch us to at least be aware of other people's points of view, even if we do not agree with them.

Your emotional health is important. Time spent having a coffee, going for a walk or getting lunch with someone you like and respect can replenish your energy and revive your mood so you feel seen, heard and brave enough to be yourself. We spend too much time with those that make us feel depleted and disrespected and this can be damaging to our thoughts and self-esteem.

We can't be what we can't see. And I don't just mean a flashy watch or an academic accolade. I am talking about being up close with people that exhibit the very best of the human experience. Those that are great advocates for others, are kind, have a strong work ethic, show vulnerability and generosity. These special individuals make us a better version of ourselves without us having to be an imitation of them.

Sharing is caring. Mutual mentoring always gives returns. Our friends and connections in our circle can model behaviours and pathways for us that we may not have thought possible. Through getting their point of view, doors can open for you that you could not have previously imagined. And you will be able to return the favour in your own way, building more appreciation and gratitude. Now THAT's a feel-good friendship.

Time is the only thing we can't make more of. Your time is precious and should be treated as such. This does not mean you have to be an arrogant nightmare to be around or hire a PA to manage your adoring fans that are hankering for your time! But you must, MUST, be discerning with it. Each time you *give it* – the clue is in the phrase – you can't get it back.

The brilliant people you seek to attract into your circle are there to serve as mutual support and evidence of what's possible. Throw yourself into connection not comparison!

The life you want to create and build for yourself will ask you to say 'no' so that you have the energy and focus to bring about the progress you seek. This means that when you are giving your attention and time to people, it has to be worth it – for them and for you.

You can find a win-win. Be discerning about the people you socialise and associate with, and in return will come the assurance and certainty that you will be stimulated, nourished and accepted. You'll always walk away from an interaction feeling energised, heard and connected with rather than drained, despondent and bored.

Consider your own metaphorical table...

Who is to be dethroned?

....

....

Who is to be promoted?

....

....

How many seats might stay empty until a worthy bottom is found to occupy them/it?

....

....

Ultimately, do the people around you represent the things you value? If they do, you're good to go and keep basking in the warm pools of pure #friendshipgoals.

If the five people you currently spend the most time with are not representative of things you love and aspire to become, or if they can keep you stuck in comparison, then you must re-evaluate.

You don't have to know each of those five people now

You may already have the personal contacts in place with someone you would like to sit in your circle. If, however, you do not yet, do not let this put you off – you can fake it till you make it.

About four years ago I was going through a particularly massive crisis of confidence having made some choices I had regretted with my business and succumbed to my predictable 'burn bright then burn out' cycle.

I had nobody at my own metaphorical table that I could rely on to be a daily cheerleader and strong presence of motivation. Of course my friends and family were behind me but they could not be at my regular beck and call due to their own busy lives. And plus, I felt like I needed to learn from, and soak up the wisdom of, a specialist expert. So, I allocated one of my empty seats to a complete stranger who was someone that I had started to binge on YouTube. His vibrancy, passion and larger-than-life personality were the breath of fresh air I needed.

His name is Gary Vaynerchuk and his videos went a long way to giving me the daily, sometimes hourly, pep talk that I needed in order to dust myself off, get up and move on from my motivation slump. I have never met him but I hope one day I get to tell him in person the influence he had on my mindset and mood. How, without knowing it, his words helped me through such a tough period in my life. I encourage you to do the same if you feel low or empty on the personal contacts you crave for your table. For example:

- If you're an artist, make a playlist of interviews with the creators you admire most and let their presence, even though remote, be around you.

- If you want to succeed in business, flood your ears with audiobooks and podcasts to hear the voices of those that have walked the path that excites you the most.

- If you seek to be the best partner you can be, again, gorge on the works of noted healers in this space, like Esther Perel – even reading a couple of pages each day will make a difference.

- Perhaps you are looking for support on your self-acceptance journey – Facebook groups or taking in the

inspiration on the #bodypositive hashtag will widen your
horizons and start to heal your relationship with yourself.

Even with those examples shared above, I get that this social
circle 'shake-up' might leave some questions around 'finding your
people' and my question back to you is 'what's the rush?'

Rather than looking to fill your chairs with urgency, take time to
integrate and enjoy the space and time you have now, thanks to your
powers of awareness and reflection. There can be a lot of new realisations to take in at this stage as some of the sands of your social
scene start to shift and new realities begin to set in.

Redefining and flourishing in our chosen social and family circles,
in non-digital spaces, can take time and adjustment. That said, and
here's where we all sigh with relief, each thought, intention and
action in support of yourself counts, no matter how small.

A bit like a snowball that gathers more icy particles as it's rolling
down a hill, all of your efforts will grow, gain momentum and take on
a life of their own in all the right ways. It is going to fall into place for
you, like it did for me.

You don't have to let go of people for good

Calling time on toxic, unsupportive, long-standing relationships, as I
said above, does not have to be done with the energy of 'burn and
destroy' but rather consideration and confidence.

The choices you are being called to make about who is in your
life at this moment might stand forever, or they could just be just for
now, serving the you that you need to be.

Perhaps, rather, you stand at a fork in the road that might mean
you are embarking on a route that will see your relationship follow
a diamond shape. Think of it this way, at the bottom point of the
diamond is the now. As you both take different routes and distance
creeps in, you will not feel as close. In the future, however, just like a
diamond's sides converge together again, so can your reconnection
further down the line.

This has happened to me numerous times over the years, especially with friendships and career connections. Some relationships that I thought I would be long and deep-rooted have faded and lost their warmth, but that is not to say they will not be ignited again. It means that, for now, we can't serve each other's needs at the same time as our own.

Some people will be in your life fleetingly, for quite a long time, or forever

I was first introduced to the teachings of Dr Iyanla Vanzant when I took part as a guest on Oprah's Life Class. She drew from her book *Acts of Faith*, and immediately helped me make sense of the shifting sands of the connections we make in our lives, highlighting that people come into our lives for 'a reason, a season, or a lifetime'.[19]

The acceptance and understanding of this concept can help us greatly in the curation of our circle to support the next phases of our lives. We simply cannot keep ties with everyone we meet and know, ad infinitum:

Those that are here for a reason are the individuals that are or were here to meet a very specific need. It might be that they were a shoulder to cry on, or someone to teach you tolerance, a mentor at a particular phase of your career or an out-on-the-town partying partner while you both searched for relationships. When your need, or the need of the other person, has been met, as brutal as it sounds, the contract is over and, as sad as it is, the relationship is complete. The reason for your connection no longer exists.

Our connections that are in our circle for a season lay deeper roots and there is more longevity to the energy exchange. These are the relationships where we grow together, see each other change and perhaps even share in each other's milestones. When these relationships come to an end, the pain can be intense. We might have come to rely on each other in some way, or perhaps it was simply expected that we would always be around for each other. Yet, just as the seasons naturally follow each other, to have summer, there must be an end to spring. You might describe these relationships as the ones that 'run their course'. These are the friendships that I have mourned the most as I have felt most invested in them, but their continuation cannot be forced on either side.

And the lifetimers will often go all the way with us. Do not be fooled into thinking these connections are formed only in our early years, although some of them are. These are the relationships that give us our most solid foundations and most significant emotional experiences. Often reserved for partners, family members and deeply significant friendships (whether made in childhood or adulthood), these individuals see us at our best and at our worst and it can sometimes feel we have a soul contract with them. These bonds are rarely broken by choice, and yet when they are, acceptance and gratitude for the experience is the path to making peace with the situation.

Phasing people out

Reflecting on who will be present on this next leg of your #comparisonfree journey will deliver you a different view on what feels possible for yourself.

That said, as I shared earlier, we do not need to approach this area with a burn-and-destroy attitude. For relationships where it feels appropriate, it can help to talk things out and share your feelings, expressing the change you would like to see. Although ultimatums rarely work, it is only fair to both parties to see if a way through can be found when the course of a relationship hits choppy waters. If you unfortunately cannot, then you can move forward from there.

This means that even though you may take yourself out of some groups, only attend compulsory family parties from now on, go silent in the group chat or simply become too busy to see the people you used to, on the whole, your absence will likely cause nothing more than a ripple.

The truth is most people don't care if you don't go to the party. I always think it is quite funny that despite how we have toiled to take on the work in our inner world, few will actually overtly notice the time, effort, love and energy we are siphoning into improving ourselves, or the changes that come with them.

And yet we are not doing it for other people, are we? They will benefit, but building the right environment for you to live #comparisonfree is, and should stay, work you do for you.

What people will notice, however, is how you walk a little taller into every room you enter, how you laugh more, have a more relaxed and flippant attitude to what you see on your phone.

They will also notice you making moves in your life, researching things you want to do and places you want to go – hatching your plans. They will also observe you expressing how you feel, your needs and your authentic thoughts, instead of staying quiet, deflecting or suppressing yourself. You are going to start to take up more space in your own world and it is safe to do so.

Working on your boundaries

That said, there might be the odd individual who makes their opinions known if they feel their relationship with you change. This is often born of a genuine longing to stay connected with you but it can be derailing all the same, for example:

- 'Why don't you hang out with us any more?'

- 'Are we not good enough for you or something?'

- 'You don't seem to be around much these days – what's going on?'

In these circumstances, personal boundaries will not only support your choices but save your life. It can feel like some people have a gravitational pull, which is trying to suck you back in and keep you in a certain pigeon hole. Their feeling better depends on preserving the status quo, so preserve it they must! But you can resist their tactics and stay true to you by being brave enough to disappoint people and reject putting their feelings and needs above our own.

Your boundaries are the way to do it and they have a special role to play when curing comparison. That is, they help us to assert ourselves, stay in our own lane and protect our time so we can invest it back into ourselves rather than fall into people-pleasing.

The use of boundaries is easy to see in the world around us. You only have to look up in a cafe to see a 'staff only' sign on a door, ropes across walkways at airports so we do not go any further, fences around properties and painted lines around car parking spaces. These significant markers help signpost environments and keep things ticking along smoothly. We all know where we are allowed to go and from where to keep our noses out.

Similarly, we each have energetic boundaries that we can access and activate to signal 'no entry!' to even the pushiest and most persistent people. So that we are following the same interpretation, your personal boundaries are energetic 'lines in the sand' that present to the world what you are available for and what you are not available for when it comes to your time, energy, emotion and attention.

Boundaries often manifest as a silent show of strength or an invisible 'do not cross' line that comes into play when you are faced with requests or demands from someone inviting you into an energy transaction. This might be quite literal with your friend that always seems to forget their wallet when you are out for dinner and you end up picking up the bill, or it might be that pushy mum at your kid's school that wants you to be present for the entire cake sale she is organising. Another example is your boss asking you to help with a task five minutes before your shift ends, knowing it will keep you late. They make the request because they think you are available for it, rightly or wrongly.

There are countless examples of boundary pushers and it can feel like they are everywhere, leaving our assertiveness reserves under pressure or empty. The result? We give away our time, effort, the potential for fun and creativity. This nibbles away at our power, making us feel like passengers in our own lives and resentful towards the people we feel are driving.

I lived most of my adult life without boundaries, going straight from uni into the schooling of the advertising industry that programmes you on day one to believe that the answer is always, always 'yes'. I was a zero boundary situation. That is until an experience of burnout forced me to make the necessary changes that still serve me well today.

So, what are the tell-tale signs that your boundaries could use a bit of work and support?

Letting people down freaks you out. When we do not have healthy boundaries, we can often be swept away by other people and their plans because we worry so much about letting them down. You believe it is much better to say 'yes' and suffer the consequences than say 'no' and risk the awkwardness. This fear of guilt overshadows your respect for yourself as you take responsibility for other people's happiness.

You feel like a doormat for other people. If there is no clear boundary for people to observe they will just assume there isn't one at all and bulldoze into your space. This can make you feel mown down and invisible in your own life, at the mercy of other people's wants and priorities.

You say 'yes' when you don't mean it and 'no' when you don't mean it. Because you want to keep the peace and not rock the boat in that one moment you say what is easiest, and yet, that decision or obligation comes around to bite you down the line.

You often make decisions that put you under strain and take months to recover from. For example, you find yourself at events that put you under financial pressure for months to follow, or at parties fake laughing at jokes that aren't funny when you would much rather be on your sofa chilling out.

You find decisions hard if not impossible. It is common for us to just draw a complete blank when we have no boundaries. Where do you want to eat tonight? Who do you want to invite? What time do we need to leave? Even the most seemingly minor decision can feel like agony as you are unclear on what works for you and why that is important to take into account.

Many of your relationships feel tricky or complicated. If our boundaries are not in place, we have no frame of reference to refer to so we cannot be consistent with our actions and behaviour. The boundary pushers LOVE this one because it means they can get away with whatever they want as you have no rules for them to follow.

You feel constantly tired and, if you're honest, a bit pissed off (and it shows!). You are so motivated by the needs of others, you leave yourself with only the crumbs from the table when it comes to time and energy that is left to invest in yourself and what you want to do. This wears you down, both physically and emotionally, and allows resentment to fester.

Ultimately, we teach people how to treat us and it is down to each of us to make sure our boundaries are clear.

Making room in our exchanges to express our own needs, feeling like other people are not in our face, as well as working our 'saying no' muscles, are crucial to having and keeping good boundaries. It's time for our next exercise . . .

> **1. How do you feel when your boundaries are being tested – be honest – write it down. If you address your boundaries those feelings will dissolve and/or massively reduce.**
>
> ....
>
> ....
>
> ....
>
> ....
>
> ....
>
> ....

2. Take an audit of your no/yes ratio

- We give away our power and burn our own boundaries when we agree to things that do not serve us. Is it any wonder you have spent no quality time at home when you have said 'yes' to every invitation to a social event and extra work project, since time began?

- When do you say, or when have you said, yes when you should have said no? What about specifics this week? List all that you can.

....

....

....

....

What were the consequences for you?

....

....

....

Putting this into practice with your comparison problems

It is possible to pull your power back and create a strategy for setting up boundaries where they matter most. Now, return to the outputs of your Unpick Your Comparison exercise from Chapter 3. In this we looked at the areas of our lives where we compare the most, defining our early memories and more recent experiences. I want you to reflect back on the four areas in which you desire to see the most growth. Pop these in the grid on the next pages to scope out the boundaries that will serve you most. I have included a couple of examples so you can apply these to your own areas of focus:

My comparison area is . . .	And when I think about my own needs, I value . . .	So, to support that I require . . .
My work.	New and fresh ideas.	Clear space in my diary and fewer calls and meetings.
My relationship.	Meaningful conversations about where we are going.	Scheduled, uninterrupted quality time.

And so I promise myself . . .	Your notes
To only commit to those that will be worth my time without exception.	
To get off my phone when we are on a date night and to stop being late to meet my partner.	

Ultimately, a big part of having good boundaries is knowing what you need in order to thrive and then organising your space and life around that so you can start getting what you need to done in order to be your whole self.

Focus on your one main thing

The strongest boundaries are those you put in place that are supported by your conviction and belief. To create these, you must know your one main thing – the real, true reason behind a decision or choice you make. This keeps you in alignment and helps you spot and connect with others that share the same driving passion for that one main thing – activism, cookery, entrepreneurship, whatever!

For example, you want to excuse yourself from your friend's hen-do in Vegas, not because you simply can't afford it. The real truth – or one main thing – is that you are more committed to being financially responsible so you can put down the deposit on a flat, which will have a life-changing impact on you and help you reach a significant goal. To say yes to the trip might put you back six months and it just isn't worth it. It will only put you back in a pattern that promotes your comparison complex.

How to say 'no' without drama

Asserting ourselves in service of our own goals takes practice and is something many of us would rather avoid. We worry if we say 'no' that we will be perceived as blunt, selfish, rude or arrogant. The hangover of guilt is also a big deterrent to speaking our truth. But when you say no with kindness and clarity on your one main thing, then it can land with ease and grace. People and situations rearrange themselves around you. For example, try these on for size:

When it comes to an invite to another tedious work party: 'I have a commitment, but thank you. Would you like me to suggest a guest in my place?'

When your friend is angling to bring her very new love interest to your wedding as their plus one: 'We've had to make so many tough decisions to get the guest-list down to size. We really can't squeeze in another guest. But I would love to have you both over for dinner soon so I can meet them.'

When your cousin nominates you to organise her over-the-top baby shower at the busiest time of your work calendar: 'I'm so flattered to be at the top of the list, which makes it all the more unfortunate I'm not in a situation where I can take this on. I'd love to support in another way – can you let me know who can take the lead instead of me and I'll pick up with them?'

Note that these responses, although applied to vastly different scenarios, share common characteristics:

They are short and to the point. Long emotive explanations are not necessary or helpful, especially when delivering challenging news. So even if you have to write down your response and then edit it, do so.

They are genuine but not too emotional. Each acknowledges that the result is perhaps not ideal for the other person and that the request is not being met. And yet, it does not overdo it.

There is no apology. After all, what do you have to apologise for? You are not in the wrong so stand in your power so you can deliver for your one main thing.

They 'land' and then move on. Because each response gets to the point and does not invite negotiation or a drawn-out conversation, it is possible to highlight the next step as the matter, as far as you are concerned, is closed.

> Think of a dilemma you currently have, or an
> invitation you don't wish to accept. How can you
> use and adapt the templates above to help you take
> yourself out of it?

You might look at the answer(s) staring back at you in the previous exercise and feel a bit nervous, and yet I am asking you to be brave and dig deep: 'This is all well and good for you, Lucy, but I could not possibly see myself doing this!' 'Jeez – this could really rattle some cages. I feel a bit scared, to be honest.'

I empathise completely. This was totally new to me too and I needed to build up the strength one 'no' at a time if I was going to release comparison's grip on me. Like any muscle, the more you use it, the stronger and more dextrous it gets. Look at this as a process of building up over time and allowing your new habits to become second nature. You will start to feel taller, bolder, more quietly confident as you benefit from the high awareness you are putting into practice.

After all, the oak tree lives within the acorn, and so your own growth will unfold.

What we have covered here in this chapter is a bit like a major health shake up for your energy and what affects your ability to show up for yourself. Key to this is your mindset and you feeding your 'good wolf' so that you can continue to work towards your own goals and desires in your own time, without the pressure to 'keep up'.

I hope this part has also released any emotional baggage that might have been holding you back so you can more forward meaningfully with compassion for yourself and others.

It bears repeating that when building the right environment for you to thrive within, transformation will be a process – but your first steps to asserting your new boundaries and being able to say no will serve you well.

CHAPTER 7

SELF-WORTH

'The worst loneliness is to not be comfortable
with yourself'
Mark Twain

As we reach the ultimate comparison cure, I want to acknowledge how far you have come. Doing this inner work is not for the feint hearted and it takes commitment and a will to live life differently – to live on your own terms.

This is a significant part of the process and is deliberately placed here as what follows will seal the deal on your ability to be less 'them' and more you. The aim is to explore how we value ourselves currently and how we can increase that value so we can go after what we want, and be able to hold it and receive it.

You will have the opportunity to better nurture your emotional health and outlook, take stock of the easy wins you can activate now for higher self-worth and also how you can love yourself hard in order to create the space to start to truly live a life aligned with you and your authentic needs and desires.

Having self-worth is knowing who you are and being OK with it. It is the result of deep inner work, increased self-care, self-love and self-acceptance. Note that possessing self-worth does not necessarily mean having to reach and retain a constant sense of joyful ecstasy, but it is at least a gentle, palpable appreciation.

It is also one of the key cornerstones of living a life free from comparison, which is why I have dedicated so much of my work, my own personal development and, indeed, this book to the topic.

But first, let us clear up some misperceptions. Having self-worth is NOT:

- to what extent do you think you are more deserving than anyone else – you are not

- being exempt from making mistakes or failing – welcome to the human race

- based on what others think about you.

To avoid any assumptions or different interpretations, and to take you deeper into your understanding, self-worth encompasses:

- how 'enough' you feel you are, just as you are

- influenced by your opinion of yourself

- what you believe you deserve

- what you believe you are ready for

- where you believe you belong (or don't belong)

- how you value yourself and show it to yourself and the world around you

- how you talk about yourself and what you feel comfortable with others saying about you.

Ultimately, self-worth is a mindset that is built on who you are as much as, if not more than, what you do. When in place and strong it will help you not only pro-actively go after the change and riches you most want to call in, but it will help you receive them, look after them and establish them.

No more easy come, easy go.

No more 'it was fun while it lasted'.

No more putting things down to luck and fluke.

Self-worth is the glue that binds our efforts and actions together like a glorious pretzel.

It will shape your days and determine your everyday experience in your love life and relationships, work and career, creativity, parenting, study, social-media likes – you name it.

I know, right?

The significance is impossible to ignore and yet, we are not striving for a light to suddenly switch on. The process of acquiring and building your sense of self-worth will see us seeking shifts and praising all progress. If you have been affected by comparing yourself to others, or fear passing on that habit to the youngsters in your life, you must learn to be aware of it and then master it.

When we are children, we each have a full tank of self-worth

Bring to mind a child that you know, or even better, think back to your earliest memories in your own childhood, when you were very young. What links us all at an early age is that we:

- **Are in full expression and completely ourselves** – singing songs, splashing in puddles, drawing pictures of imaginary lands, saying our thoughts aloud because it was important for people to know which dinosaur was our second favourite.

- **Will take what we want** – food off other people's plates, toys from the toy box, too much space in our parents' beds whilst they appeased us in order to get at least some sleep.

- **Try and try again** – falling off our bikes, climbing the tree in the park, pronouncing the words we could not quite get right. Taking a tumble was just part of life and we had the bumps and grazes to prove it.

- **Love our bodies** – running around in only a nappy, wearing all of our favourite clothes at one time because, why not? Playing with our toes and sliding down the stairs on our bottoms, just totally at ease with what we looked like and what we were able to do.

- **Are shown important tasks that help us fit into society** – how to answer the phone, how to use a knife and fork, use the toilet, cross the road, all fairly practical, and yet, all help us with our development without any hidden agendas or motivations.

- **Ask questions** – Where do babies come from? Why does that person smell? Our curiosity was unbridled, persistent and innocent. We knew what we didn't know and this was no cause for fear, worry or humiliation.

- **Know our needs because they came from within us.** Hungry? Too hot? Too cold? Need a hug? Then make it clear and let it be known so that need can be met.

As we get older and we start to have more exposure to the world, things begin to change. Our inherent self-worth and ease with the world come under threat through some very specific shifts.

- **We start to compare ourselves** – ranking against and competing with others in order to measure our own growth.

- **We place success and importance on the things outside ourselves** – like possessions, people we know, qualifications, job titles, status updates, social-media followers and so on.

- **'No Biggy'** – we stifle, hide and suppress our feelings or needs in order not to upset or inconvenience someone else. We choose not to say 'that's not OK' even when people are rude, out of order, disrespectful or downright malicious towards us.

- **We encounter feedback and sometimes even bullying behaviour from others** – that is intended to get us to act, speak or behave a certain way – the way *they* want. This can then degenerate into outsourcing our decisions to others.

- **We develop 'imposter syndrome'** – that is, despite our experience, potential, skills and talents we feel we are not qualified, able or worthy enough to 'do the thing'. This might be to take the job role, give a talk at a local group, or write a blog post on a subject, for fear of being found out, named, shamed and humiliated.

- **We compile evidence against ourselves** – instead of taking the learning from each tumble and adjusting our technique as we did when we were children, we instead focus on where we have fallen short and collect reasons we cannot be or do the feat in question.

> *'Hold the hand of the child that lives in your soul.*
> *For this child, nothing is impossible'*
> – Paulo Coelho

We store memories and experiences from our childhood or formative years within us and these will have led us to believe the world is a certain way, what life is like for 'people like us' and what you need to say and do to survive in your close community group and family set up.

When we talk about the 'inner child' state that we each possess, it is, ultimately, an accumulation of past pain that stems from the fact that at some point, in one or various ways, our need for love, acceptance, nurturing and understanding were not met when we were children.

Speak to your inner child to help the adult you are today

The challenge to us as grown-ups is, if left unacknowledged and unhealed, that these negative experiences can be a persistent trigger. This can knock our progress and cause us to act out like we did at the time, when we might have been nine years old.

We simply can't get in a time machine and go back in history and what might have happened to us can never be reversed. And yet we can look to heal our inner child today and soothe and take care of those needs in the present moment and in the future.

To share an example of this in action let me share one of my areas of inner-child healing. Growing up, I remember being told to be quiet and 'stop being a show off' out of the blue by an important person in my life. Just like I touched on earlier in the book, I soon attached myself to the false belief that speaking up and saying what I thought was not right and made me unlikeable. So, I learned to copy other people who might have been not so vociferous and 'toned it down a bit'.

Fast forward to adulthood and my inner child has been, and is, triggered in a number of ways:

- When I receive unsolicited feedback about my words
  or deeds not being to the liking of someone. I'm not
  talking about being called out about being wrong, that is
  necessary for my growth. I mean more like, 'I wouldn't have
  done it this way . . .' or, 'It's a shame you did it like that . . .'
  These are subjective opinions that I didn't ask for and I am
  not that interested in, to be honest. They're designed to
  limit me just as the comments in my childhood were.

- If I perceive someone else living fully in their expression and being rewarded for it, that will also trigger a reaction as it brings up memories from my past when I chose not to pursue opportunities because it would mean using the qualities within me that I believed people did not want to see. A perfect example of this is my own bugbear I shared with you from when I saw that an entrepreneur I follow had been invited to do another TEDx Talk. My blood boiled to see his social media announcement. My inner child was so distraught at feeling overlooked again that I could not see this as inspirational information.

When I revisit the original memory, my feelings feel intense and vivid even though the memory is nearly thirty years old. When triggered I am taken right back there, and it has been such fuel for my comparison tendency.

Just as the future self-visualisation/journaling exercise helped you connect with your potential, future power and aspiration in Chapter 3, this next guided exercise will help you access the sacred information that your inner child would like to gift you in order to heal.

To complete this exercise use a notepad and journal to capture the thoughts, feelings, answers, impulses and visions that come up for you. As always, go with your FIRST instinct, do not let your intellectual mind drown out a message from your soul and/or deep subconscious.

Firstly, set the intention that you are going to meet your inner child – don't obsess about the exact age group or life stage you were at – you can do this numerous times and receive golden insight you can act on and integrate.

Now imagine...

You approach your inner child who is playing in an area familiar to you – perhaps a garden, school playground, a classroom . . .

You say hello and your inner child greets you in return.

You look into the eyes of your inner child.

What are they feeling towards you at this moment? Are they shy? Excited? Quiet? Energetic? Curious? Perhaps a bit nervous?

You sit down quietly with them, putting them at ease and respecting their space, mirroring their body language.

Do they shake your hand? Sit on your lap? Or simply carry on playing, maintaining space between you? Let the rest unfold – there is no need to judge.

You next ask, 'How are you feeling today? I am here to make sure you get the care, guidance and love you deserve. What do you need most right now?' The answer may come in words, a picture, a gesture, an emotion, a knowing feeling. This might vary depending on the age of your inner child that you are meeting today.

What is their response? Be open to all insights, no matter how unclear they seem at first.

Act exactly as you would with another child at this age, create space for them, gently look to understand, let them feel heard without interruption, ask questions that intuitively come up for you.

Let them feel the love you have for them. You might like to share with them how much you love and care for them, and wish them to be cared for. If your inner child wishes to be cradled, hugged, or held, embrace the opportunity.

Once you feel you have made the connection with your inner child, you can visualise yourself walking back into your house. Focus on your breathing, stretch your body, and open your eyes.

This activity may bring up some uncomfortable feelings or painful memories and it is not intended to replace therapy. The insight, however, can provide the first steps to nourishing and restoring those parts of ourselves that might be sabotaging our thoughts, limiting our behaviours and allowing comparison to play havoc with the choices we make and how we show up for ourselves. It allows us to take responsibility in a non-judgemental way.

How can you look after your inner child going forward?

This can feel like deep work. This exercise particularly can unearth some unknown perspectives that might make us feel a bit fragile and yet at the same time I have always been left with a great sense of relief. It is as though, through these prompts, I am given hints as to how I can best protect my heart and give myself what I need as an adult today.

Building self-worth and staying stocked up

One of the tragic things about self-worth is that, over time, it can drain away and before we know it we feel like we have absolutely nothing left within us. On darker days, even feeling slightly better seems impossible.

I look at it as if it were a warm bath. When you are in a state of self-acceptance, it is warming, calming and stimulates your senses. But sometimes we accidentally pull the plug out and we are left cold and shivery and it is too late, or too much has been lost to get topped up again.

There is no such thing as 'too late', so let's just park that belief here. This next section is full of pointers you can activate in your own life in order to notice where your self-worth might be suffering so you can stop the sleepwalking in your life, for the benefit of you and everyone you love most.

The clues are there for us to find. Where we shrink or hide ourselves in our everyday life is a representation of where we are not feeling worthy. These are often plain to see in the standards we set for ourselves and ask other people to meet.

We teach people how to treat us and your presentation of yourself will influence your experience of the world. Note, this does not mean meeting archaic, thin and white-centric beauty standards of photo-shopped 'perfection'. Nor does it mean you have to spend money that could be used elsewhere in your life to binge on items that you think you need to have.

This is about feeling good enough. Showing up as your best self in your life, ready to receive the rewards, opportunities and experiences to match that.

So, if I were to ask you whether you are an old banger or a magnificent machine, what would your answer be?

Humour me as I share this analogy . . . Imagine you are driving around a car park and it is really busy. There are lots of cars around as you twist and turn your vehicle, looking for space. You see a free spot beside an old banger of a vehicle. The bumper is hanging off, there are scratches and damaged paintwork and one of the doors is a different colour. Plus, it's parked wonky across the lines. The owner clearly does not take care of it, how it is driven or what it looks like.

You realise it will be tight to get your car in the spot next to it but, to be honest, so what if you do scrape the doors? They will never know as it's nearly a wreck anyway, what is one more bash?

You complete your errands and you come back to your car. This time, there is a luxury car with a custom-colour paint job parked behind you. The windows sparkle, the sumptuous leather seats look better than those in your actual home and the metal work adorning the vehicle could be mistaken for fine art pieces. It's a vision to behold! Until your bubble of admiration is burst by the realisation that you will need to reverse towards it in order to get out!

You are going to have to be so, so careful, space conscious and alert so you do not touch that car – it would be more than your life is worth. Clearly, the owner is very driven (excuse the pun!), discerning and successful to have a car like that.

Compare your attitude to how you regard the first car – the old banger – versus the second one – the posh wheels. Same car park and the same mundane task of parking, and yet, a completely different outlook and approach! All too often, too many of us are showing up in life as the old banger.

How we look at ourselves, what we say about and to ourselves, and how we present to the world are sending messages that say, 'I don't value myself, so you don't have to either!' Now, fair enough, for many of us our destiny is not to be a *James Bond* supercar, but we can do a lot better in the care we invest in ourselves. When we do, just like the parking story, life treats us differently and we experience better and improved behaviour from people.

It has nothing to do with chasing status and everything to do with showing up as our best selves and displaying our self-worth.

Your self-worth glow-up: take a personal audit

Without judgement, bring to mind and journal some of the ways that you compromise and this will give you a clue that your self-worth has gone AWOL. There are some prompts below you are encouraged to consider.

Do you accept the worst table at a restaurant, because 'it will be fine' and you don't want to cause a fuss? Perhaps you take the table situated by the loo, which is directly by the dirty crockery station, when a simple request could see you sat with a view to die for in the buzz of the main room.

What is the state of your underwear drawer? This one always makes people cringe. You do not need to have a million matching pairs of La Perla knickers and yet so many of us have the most shameful underwear situation, with holes, faded colours, loose string and all sorts happening. When you open that part of your drawer you want to feel 'yes!' I know when I am not on top of my game as my pants always tell me!

Are your bath towels inherited from your granny? Yeah, OK, when you move out of home every little helps and why have the expense of stocking up on bathroom supplies? And yet, as a hard-working adult who is trying to live their best life, don't you think it's time you upgraded to a fluffy, pristine, not hard and scratchy towel to use every day? The same goes for your bed linen – treat yourself to a beautiful set that is your choice and all of your own. You don't need that old, crusty energy in your life.

Do you have the crap chair at work? How and where you sit to work should not be a cause of pain, discomfort and strife. If your chair or other resources at work have a 'knack' you need to know and use in order for them to function, then get rid of them! You deserve comfort and a basic standard of utility so you can do and be your best. This is not an acceptable compromise.

What does your toothbrush and hairbrush say about you? If they are old, overused and you would be embarrassed for someone to catch a view of them then it is time for an upgrade in this department. Your basic hygiene standards are not up for discussion. Neither brush needs to be top of the range and expensive but they should not be a health hazard.

Do you never leave enough time to be on time? Do you depart your home for work or have to dash to appointments and meetings under a personal bombardment of expletives because, 'Oh shit! Is that the time?' This is not about being the punctuality police and yet your time, as well as other people's, is important. It is a sign of how 'with it' and 'together' you are and if you can be one thing – be reliable. Being seen as someone who is nonchalant or chaotic does your personal brand, and your nervous system, no favours.

Do you think it's OK to turn up with wet hair? It isn't – we are not in a gym changing room or post-swimming lessons at school. A person that knows and shows their self-worth is prepared and presentable and dry to the touch.

Do you have a 'for best' rule on some things? Do you have an expensive perfume that sits full on your dresser and has done for years, or gorgeous premium underwear (again with the pants, Lucy?!), clothes, knives and forks, paper, scented candles, etc. Whatever you keep and preserve for best, review how savvy that actually is. OK, I can appreciate perhaps only rarely wearing fancy jewellery that is a family heirloom but for the rest, come on! Wear it, light it, spray it and use it . . . this is your one life!

And now over to you . . .

Which of the habits highlighted above do you resonate
with?

....

....

....

....

....

What other patterns, and quirks, similar to the above
are sparking your awareness that you are not treating
yourself as though you are worthy?

....

....

....

....

....

How else do you tolerate unnecessary, unhelpful
compromise?

....

....

....

....

....

How do you show yourself that you are not enough?

....

....

....

....

....

What things in your home, wardrobe and environment are tatty, need fixing, simply do not work?

....

....

....

....

....

Bearing in mind your answers above, and your desire to shift to a better, stronger state of self-worth, where can you upgrade and inject quality and beauty into your life, no matter how small?

....

....

....

....

....

Now, having completed this exercise, please don't despair at the state of some of your self-worth indicators. As I have said before, this is a process, so you do not need to get yourself into debt or completely transform yourself overnight. Let's look to achieve positive increments.

The more you love yourself the more worthy you will feel

It might feel like you are having to do a lot for yourself as part of this comparison curing process. I am not going to apologise for consistently asking you to dig deep because it is important that you take radical responsibility in your own life. But you do not have to be harsh on yourself – being compassionate to yourself will allow you to be even more authentically you.

Self-love is a word and concept that can be easily misunderstood and is often distilled down to simply having an early night or eating expensive chocolate! I am a big fan of both of these but we can, and should, harness its deeper properties: an overt and deep appreciation of ourselves, our journey and our progress today.

For this next technique I will borrow from the bookshelves of love and relationship coaches, in particular, the work of Dr Gary Chapman and his definition of 'love languages'. As Dr Chapman outlines, love languages are the ways in which we express and receive love and these in turn influence how our hearts feel and whether we feel like we are fully loved.

Clues to our identifying own love languages lie in pondering what made you feel the most loved as a child? Or when you really want to show someone you care about them, what first comes to your mind as a way to display your affection and appreciation?

According to Dr Chapman, there are five love languages (ways to express, interpret and receive love) that each of us will resonate with on a different level:

1. **Words of affirmation . . .** I feel most cared for when a partner is open and expressive giving me compliments; telling me how brilliant they think I am, how much they appreciate me, etc.

2. **Quality time . . .** I feel the most love when a partner and I are together, fully present and engaged in what we're doing, whether that's at the shops, sitting at home or on a date.

3. **Giving of gifts . . .** I get all the good feels when a partner takes the time to give me a present.

4. **Acts of service . . .** I really value a partner doing me favours and relieving me of tasks, like doing the laundry or looking after the dog, so I can go and see a friend.

5. **Physical touch/affection . . .** I feel most loved when hugging, kissing, touching, and enjoying other kinds of physical intimacy.[20]

> **Having reviewed these descriptions, what do you feel is your love language?**
>
> ....

So, here's this thing, it's all very well a partner knowing and acting on your love language, but how regularly do you speak this language to yourself? How often do you show yourself love in the way that touches you the most, and you feel it vibrate in your system most freely?

When trying to reduce our comparison tendency, a golden tip is to start replenishing yourself, appreciating what you have and acknowledging who you are through giving yourself what you need. Ultimately, the aim is to fill up your cup of self-worth by truly loving yourself. After all, who else is going to consistently do it for you, if you don't?

Below are some direct action tips to help you activate this incredible self-love tool to keep your spirits and motivation high. If your love language is:

Words of affirmation . . . Make sure each day you have a running monologue of positive comments going. Set notifications on your phone to pop up with a ping of nourishing reminders and pep talks.

Quality time . . . Block out space in your diary just for you to rest, relax or simply do something you love. Go to a lunchtime concert, book a spa day or light a candle and read a book in silence.

Giving of gifts . . . Buy yourself flowers once a week. Choose a bi-yearly birthday gift to invest in yourself with a present to cherish.

Acts of service . . . Think about how you can remove the hassle from your day through delegating or bringing in a bit of support. For example, if you can, get a cleaner to help with your household chores or book a taxi to your friend's party so you can have a couple of drinks and not have to drive.

Physical touch/affection . . . After each shower, take your time to really massage your moisturiser into your skin. Don't be afraid to regularly invest in self pleasure, for example buying clothes that feel good next to your skin.

Connecting with yourself via the relevant language regularly can keep your inner fire burning and the self-love flowing, so you can feel emotionally strong and create the life which feels like the perfect fit for you, no longer affected by comparison.

Accepting appreciation even if it makes you cringe

Oh boy. The biggy. Were you hoping I wasn't going to bring this up? Do you feel like you want to curl up and die or run away when someone says something nice to you, acknowledges your presence, expresses their thanks or points to your achievements? I know this might be making your skin crawl at the very thought.

Many of us are artful in avoiding and swerving compliments when we:

- deflect the words coming our way a bit like swatting a fly – 'get them away from me!'

- quickly reciprocate, a bit like throwing a hot potato – 'Oh no, your cake was delicious too!'

- play down the interaction to reduce its significance – 'Really? This old thing? I'm surprised it even fits any more!'

How does receiving compliments make you feel?

....

....

....

How often do you ignore or forget your efforts and accomplishments?

....

....

....

Being able to accept a compliment is the hallmark of someone who knows their worth. A puppy doesn't die if you receive a compliment, so we need to stop acting like it. You won't turn into an arrogant nightmare. You won't become reliant on them in order to feel good. And you won't stop being a good person.

It is not just a nice thing to do, so you don't hurt the feelings of the person complimenting you. By hearing, knowing and seeing the good in yourself you weaken the comparison voice and it opens your heart to who you are seen as today, allowing you to see more value in yourself and the contribution you are making in the world around you.

I find this is such a sticking point for my clients, and yet, the damaging habit of swerving compliments can be dissolved with a simple phrase, which is, 'Thank you!'

For those that would like to take the practice deeper, you can also mix things up with:

'That is so kind of you to say – thank you', and also 'I receive that kindness so gratefully' – a compliment is a gift after all, so why not treat it as such?

If you can start this one thing today, you will be amazed at how many more good words and positive opportunities start to flood your way. You are demonstrating your openness to receive what life is trying to give you when you show you know your worth.

The power of receiving

'New level. New devil'

– Joyce Meyer

By this point in my comparison cure client programme, people are starting to feel very different about what their life can be because their present is actively transforming in front of them (and that's not just their underwear drawer!).

The people or things that used to trigger comparison, and with that self-judgement, self-criticism and self-hatred, just don't have the same effect any more. Replaced by focus, confidence and self-belief, the world, although to the untrained eye may look exactly the same, is different, changed forever in immeasurable ways.

It's like they have graduated to a new video-game level, having worked, fought and stuck at completing the tests of the previous one. And although there is, of course, nothing to fear and everything to play for, this is where the wobbles can start to set in.

This is why this next part of our journey requires your awareness and serious consideration – this will make or break your ability to stay on this positive run of self-care and self-development.

With this new level – indeed a new chapter of your life – no matter your age or background, will come new experiences and new challenges. So, we need to work on your muscles of receiving, the prime of which are sophisticated forms of self-sabotage: 'upper limit problems' and resistance to the abundance that you have been attracting into your life as a result of your commitment to your own path.

What is an upper limit problem or ULP? It was Gay Hendricks who coined the phrase in his book *The Big Leap* [21] – his name might ring a bell as I previously highlighted his book in Chapter 5 when exploring the unexpected fear of success.

The book holds incredible insight and applicable tools and 'a-ha' moments, so it's worth your time to digest in full, but essentially, Hendricks teaches that each of us has an internal thermostat [22] that sets the temperature in our lives for how much success, wealth, happiness, love, and affection we can allow in. That level or 'temperature' is our individual upper limit setting. A bit like a comfort zone for our achievement that we can reach without overheating or malfunctioning.

Taking this further, this can mean people are not able to receive all the good things that life is presenting because these feel unfamiliar and they do not feel worthy of having them. The positive things are 'too hot' for their internal thermostat and it starts to creak and malfunction under the pressure. This then triggers hidden sabotaging tendencies, and these serve as obstacles to long-term success and fulfilment.

Humans, it turns out, are not particularly good at being at peace and we find the smooth running and consistent comfort in life, ironically, uncomfortable – it challenges our limits.

To share an example: I coached someone whose discomfort and low self-worth applied to her finances. She wanted to save for an adventure abroad and yet would reach a certain number in her bank account and then go for an almighty online binge, shopping for things she didn't really want or need. She felt such resistance to how possible this trip could be that she would damage her means to make it happen.

We don't believe we deserve to be happy all the time, so we cap our levels of joy for no reason.

Another case of Upper Limit Problems showed up with a client of mine in her relationship. She found whenever things were bobbing along smoothly with her bae she would start an argument and it would interrupt and end the period of harmony they had been enjoying. Once she hit her ceiling of the love she was accustomed to experiencing, she spun out of control.

Does this resonate with you?

- Have you reached certain wellbeing goals, achieving great results, and then gone back to destructive habits, even though you were starting to see exactly the results you had been hoping for?

- Have you found yourself close to having success with your blog only to find an excuse not to keep writing? Even though the feedback was so great you almost couldn't believe it?

- Perhaps you started getting lots of green lights in your business? Attracting amazing press coverage and clients. But you started avoiding replying to emails and cancelling meetings. Even though those KPIs were the exact measures you set out to achieve.

We self-sabotage to take ourselves backwards and down to what we feel are more familiar surroundings. Because of our low sense of self-worth, we just cannot seem to receive the size of, or sustain the time span of, the new happy experience.

Breaking destructive patterns so you can move on and move up

Self-sabotaging can and does lead to destructive cycles of success-crash-success-crash, and so the pattern continues . . . until, of course, it doesn't because you start paying attention and taking action accordingly!

So how do we 'hold the stare' with these innate, subconscious habits that could bring our dreams down like a house of cards if we are not aware of them? We must increase our capacity for success and happiness.

Put simply, just like reaching any summit or surviving new and radical environments, you must acclimatise. You must grow and expand to the size of the gifts you want to attract. Think of it this way, imagine that you and I wanted to climb Everest (I mean, how hard can it be?!). We would not grab a couple of meal deals from the local shop, whiz to the airport, put our big coats on and head for the hills to the chants of 'Everest, here we come!'

No way. On setting our goal we would prepare for the trip carefully, gather what we needed and take considered steps to get to the first base camp. There we would dwell as our eyes adjusted to the light, our skin adapted to the cold and our lungs learned to function at altitude on that trusty plateau.

As each of these crucial new functions integrated into our physical bodies, we would take our time, running tests and gathering strength to make the next ascent to the next base camp, on the way towards our summit. On completion of that acclimatisation then, and only then, is it time to get up, go higher and do more.

Similar to the hypothetical (and thankfully-never-going-to-happen expedition) highlighted above, in order for our own success and happiness to stick around, integrate and last, we too need to acclimatise.

In real life terms, this shows up as the following:

When you get a big invoice paid to the business and your bank account looks really healthy. Once you have covered your bills, instead of binge spending on investments that are not a priority, let the rest of the money sit and rest in your account. Even though it might be more than you have earned before or had in your account for a long time. Take time to be at that new, higher limit that you are worthy of rather than sabotage yourself and reverting to comfortable, old patterns. You don't need to buy that sofa, even though you can. Rather, make a decision in line with high self-worth and show the universe you can hold on to £5 and it will send you £50. Show it you can hold onto £50 and soon it will be £500 . . . Show your money that it's safe with you and more of it will hang around more often. Prove to yourself that you have the capacity to retain more wealth.

When you are in a loving partnership and you are in a happy phase. Things have been good, no, great actually, for a good stretch of time and you can't remember the last time you and your partner butted heads. This can set off your upper limit alarms – you start to feel nervous in this new territory, which is so unfamiliar. The old you might revert to sending a bitchy text to them to start some drama as has been your previous unconscious habit. Instead, journal on your feelings in a notebook and let the moment pass, let the love flow to you as it wants to! Sail past that upper limit and show your capacity to receive more love for longer periods of time. You will be able to bask in the warm currents of a healthy, adult relationship for as long as feels right because you know you are worth it.

I come up against my own ULPs fairly regularly when my dreams start showing up, presenting evidence that they are coming true. Like writing this book, for example! To get through these damaging tendencies I have a go-to toolbox of techniques that means I don't resort to drama, avoidance and denial (my own self-sabotaging behaviours). Instead, these allow me to just go with it so I cannot only get my heart's desire, I can keep it.

How to work through, and graduate past an ULP:

- **Pause and take stock** in order to allow yourself to celebrate your new view. Put your fingers on your pulse and rub your heart to alleviate any anxious or unfamiliar feelings in the moment. Remember, this is not a trick.

- **Accept and expect that you will feel uncomfortable as you grow** – set an internal alert system for an upper limit problem when things are going well, and what you want is showing up in your life.

- **Let yourself grow** to the size of the life you want to experience. Increase your capacity for how great you are willing to let it be by nourishing what you have and taking care of it. Practise gratitude and keep up with your evidence journal – you can get and keep your version of happiness.

- **Talk it out with someone you trust** – I am known for my long voicemails across various apps. In an ULP moment, I will reach for my phone and usually head to my chat with my friend Gail. It goes a bit like this: 'I just want to let you know that I am ULPing right now – is it OK if I talk it out and get the words out of my system? I recognise this is happening . . . I am uncomfortable because . . .' Even if it's a 30-second voicemail nobody will ever get around to listening to, it will soothe and stop the sabotaging.

- **Remember it's just one moment** – know that your ability to bear discomfort and awkwardness is a sign you are pushing through the upper limit and you will not be sucked into sabotaging practices or old comparison patterns.

● **Breathe and take a beat** – if you catch yourself about
  to start an argument, daydreaming about a disaster that
  shows no signs of occurring, or you are about to make an
  impulsive and rash business decision, take some big belly
  breaths and then . . . don't. Do something completely
  different and grounding – sort your laundry, go out and
  run an errand, dance to your favourite song in order to
  help the moment pass.

I urge you to look back at your own goals that we started out with
in Chapter 3 and look at what those achievements can bring to your
life.

Reviewing how you are feeling about your progress in your work and personal life, when do Upper Limit Problems tend to crop up for you?

....

....

....

....

....

When confronted with the next growth opportunity that presents itself to you, will you pass the assignment? Which tip above will you use?

....

....

....

....

....

How will these tips help you push through to another new level and receive what is being held in trust for you?

....

....

....

....

....

We will tend to self-sabotage based on our sense of self-worth. So, the more worthy of love, abundance, opportunities and joy we feel, the less we will be prone to self-sabotage and vice versa. Through bringing our awareness to our limits and capacity to experience the big, bold, authentic lives we are here to lead, we can gradually work at dissolving these old limits and in doing so expand to our unique, personal, cannot-be-imitated potential. This is where we reach a zone of being completely ourselves, with comparison rarely – if ever – getting a look in.

I'll share these words:

> *'Our deepest fear is not that we are inadequate.*
> *Our deepest fear is that we are powerful beyond measure'*
> – Marianne Williamson

Having taken part in this intense study of your own self-worth, I hope you are feeling a boost to your awareness in how you might have put up barriers to feeling worthy up to now.

Clients often find that through making the specific tweaks and changes, this part of the process feels like opening a window and letting the fresh air rush in due to the immediate shifts it can create. One realisation is often that we have the power to give ourselves what we need rather than having to wait to be given it by someone else.

With this said, I ask that you are especially gentle with your heart at this stage before you look at consolidation as making new patterns and mindsets takes time. This is deep work that you have undertaken and I am so proud of you for it.

PART THREE

BE HEALTHY

CHAPTER 8

LIVING
#COMPARISONFREE

'I think that little by little I'll be able to solve my
problems and survive'
Frida Kahlo

At the temple of Apollo at Delphi, the place the Ancient Greeks thought was the centre of the world, there is an engraving in the original Greek that reads: 'Know thyself'. Socrates later expanded this to: 'The unexamined life is not worth living'.

At this stage, as we look to complete our time together for now, it is fair to say there has been some pretty intense examination going on. There is not much of your inner or outer world that has been left untouched, unobserved and unquestioned in your own quest to cure your comparison.

Over the course of this journey, if you are similar to my clients or workshop guests, you may have laughed, cried, felt uncomfortable, felt relief, experienced both the 'ouch' and the 'a-ha!' moments. Regardless, my hope is that you have come to know yourself better and will continue to examine, explore and resist how our environment and programming conspire to create and then establish our comparison mindset.

Welcome to the home straight

This book and this work are designed to shake things up in your life and wake you up to your own gifts, talents and resources as well as the ways that you might knock yourself off the pony.

Ultimately, the new self-focus, self-confidence and self-worth that will be building within you hold the keys to your immunisation against comparison.

This closing chapter contains the important tools, practices and provisions that successful #comparisonfree candidates all have in place to help them stay in their own lane for good. These are designed to focus more on your day-to-day life, to reinforce and support the mindset changes and shifts that will be happening due to your different outlook.

I promised you a truth serum in the opening paragraphs of this book and just in case you start to fall into old habits, here is a recap with some essential reminders 'at a view' in case you feel yourself straying away from your truth and need to hit the panic button.

Your diagnosis:

FROM CHAPTER 1: GETTING INTIMATE WITH YOUR COMPARISON CONDITION

- Keep an eye on your Comparison Trigger Indicators (CTI) – if you notice them coming back, go immediately to your values and goals to remind yourself of your own path.

- The same applies if you are measuring yourself against other people, whether you know them or not.

- Stay aware of how your personality traits might pose an obstacle to you understanding situations and use your super powers regularly (no cape necessary!).

- Know that your comparison is trying to reveal a crystal of insight to you – don't dwell in jealousy, move through it and move on!

FROM CHAPTER 2: UNDERSTANDING WHO YOU ARE

- Stay checked-in with how you are showing up authentically and letting the real you lead in your life.

- Refer back to the prompts when it comes to what's true for you, how you act, how you feel and what you say.

- Reconnect with your True You Guide as often as you can and put to use the insights that that special guiding force holds in trust for you. By rubbing your heart, you can immediately stimulate the power within.

- Allow yourself to want what you want based on what truly stirs and motivates you – don't give in to the pressure to be positive all the time.

FROM CHAPTER 3: UNDERSTANDING WHAT YOU WANT

- Remember that your success is yours and yours alone to define.

- Inherited goals, or outdated, ones will not serve you in the long run. Instead, work towards being led by your values every day.

- You can revisit the Unpick Your Comparison resource at any time as new and more ways of comparing present themselves to you – use those crystals of insight to guide your next right steps.

- Keep your compass word close and let it help you stay the course as you work towards your own version of happiness and success.

- Don't forget to tap into the powers of your imagination and visualisation – make your vision board and refer to it often. The same goes with looking at your perfect day and how you can activate that now.

- You have your own goals laid out now so make sure you are tracking your progress with these and make tweaks as you need to – this will keep you firmly in your own lane.

Your remedies:

FROM CHAPTER 4: FOCUS

- Remember to stay really focused on you as you are now and don't be tempted to compare to your past self.

- Remain conscious of where your precious resource of time goes so you can contain your energy and stay energised, rather than leaking it everywhere!

- Arrange the start and end of your weekdays so they support your mood and melt away distraction and unhelpful thoughts.

- Try not to get caught up in perfection and know that some progress is better than no progress!

- You have more to play with than you think right now so use and leverage your resources to propel yourself forward and keep on track.

- Get your digital life organised and managed so it is an entertaining and informative presence rather than a distracting one.

- Remove clutter and therefore stagnancy in your living space so the right energy can flow and you have the physical and mental space to thrive and stay focused.

FROM CHAPTER 5: SELF-CONFIDENCE

- Be aware that success and making progress can be uncomfortable and we can assign negative beliefs that hold us back. It is SAFE for you to grow and prosper.

- Stay close to your own picture of confidence and allow yourself to go up and down the scale. There are no such things as bad days.

- You can tweak and build your confidence at any time through your words, approach and actions. Arrive at your combination and keep showing up for yourself and the life you want to lead.

FROM CHAPTER 6: BUILDING THE RIGHT ENVIRONMENT

- There is enough to go around – a win for someone else does not mean a loss for you.

- Get your mindset straight and power up your positivity knowing that you can trust the timing of your life.

- Look around you – there are different success stories everywhere and it is never too late to make peace with what might have held you back and move forward with grace.

- Swap imitation for inspiration and be aware of the tribute act tendency.

- You may have to switch up your social circle in order to elevate yourself to meet the life you want to create. Be discerning and apply your awareness so you are lifted up and positively influenced.

- Imagine your table and curate its participants so your environment thrives knowing you can do this in a drama-free way.

- Practise keeping good boundaries and saying no so you can make meaningful progress in your own way.

FROM CHAPTER 7: SELF-WORTH

- Your opinion of yourself and the worth you feel is a powerful tool – cultivate it.

- Your inner child holds information that can help you be the grown up you want to be – listen with compassion to what it has to say.

- You can see signs of your self-worth reflected in your life all around you – take stock regularly and make upgrades accordingly.

- The more you love yourself, the more worth you feel so identify your love language and apply it in your life.

- Work on your ability to receive what the world wants to give you from compliments, to money, to opportunities – stay open to them all.

🌸 This process will stir up your self-sabotaging habits – we all
have them. Be mindful of these patterns so you can push
through those imaginary limits and reach for the sky.

🌸 It's not your inadequacy that scares you, it's your power!

Your new normal – beware the double punch

*'Watch your thoughts, they become your words; watch your
words, they become your actions; watch your actions, they
become your habits; watch your habits, they become your
character; watch your character, it becomes your destiny'*

– Lao Tzu

One of the best things about self-help and the growth that comes
with it is that we learn what works for us, we do it more and things feel
good more often. That said, the flip side is that if we have an off day
we chastise and judge ourselves, which serves as a double punch!

'Oh, gah! I looked at where they are going on holiday today and
I still haven't hit my savings plan target! Why can't I get my stuff
together – I am such a loser.' That's one punch!

Followed by, 'But oh ahhh! I know I shouldn't be comparing! I
feel so bad, I was such a bitch about them and their holiday!' – the
second punch!

The same goes for when you have been on a really good run of
expressing yourself and are feeling the benefits of good boundaries,
then suddenly you find yourself backed into a corner because you
said 'yes' to your pushy colleague on the spur of the moment.

On the road to a #comparisonfree life, these things happen! It just
means we were slow to spot the 'test' or assignment and respond in
the optimum way.

Having a blip or a less than one hundred per cent record does
NOT mean you have had an unsuccessful day. As part of this
programme we are aiming to escape the negative cycle of highs and
lows, or peaks and troughs, because of the intense and unruly effects

of comparison. Rather, we are aiming to establish a new normal, and, to continue the helpful visual analogy of a graph, we are looking to achieve a shallow, wobbly line. A bit like delicate ripples on the water – there is undulation that we can flow with, rather than be given the emotional whiplash of the former.

Sarah Powell, founder of the concept of Self-Celebration, calls it 'No bad days', and there is such power and beauty in that simplicity. Always aim for progress, not perfection, and get as close as you can, as often as you can, to the ideal habits and behaviours that serve you. There are no bad days!

Asking for help

You are strong.
You have what it takes.
You are capable.
You have potential.

All of these things, I know to my bones, are true about you.

And you also don't have to walk your path alone. It is possible to receive support along the way and still be doing the work and still maintain your independence.

I used to have such a martyr complex and would shoulder pressure and responsibility like it was a badge of honour. It never brought me anything apart from borderline adrenal fatigue. For me, asking for help, assistance or favours used to be a sign of weakness or – even worse – a sign I was not coping with my lot, even though the truth is that I rarely perform well under the strain. I turn into the living embodiment of the clenched-teeth emoji!

It was when I realised how much I was slowing myself down and making things so much harder than they had to be that I changed my relationship with asking for help or a favour. Gradually, I was able, with trepidation and butterflies in my tummy, to start to receive what I needed and wanted without strife or struggle. It didn't always work, but even the gesture made me feel brave and gave me the boost I needed.

Now I am the queen of asking. There is nothing too big or out of reach that I wouldn't have a go at these days. Partly because I feel when my heart is in the right place, what will be will be. And the other big element is I am not overly attached to a finite or single result.

When we ask for help, we create a slipstream for progress and we can meet our dreams halfway.

Here are the principles to the perfect ask, whether you need a favour from a close friend, want to propose to your partner, ask for a deadline extension, or you want a meeting with a budget holder at a big corporate company, some or all of these will apply.

Zero entitlement. The most important thing to do in order to get the very best result is to clean up your energy. What this means is you must rid yourself and 'the ask' of any sense of entitlement that you might have towards the thing or result you're asking for. No matter what your reasons may be. You might deserve the pay rise, your podcast may be really popular and you might even have been on TV. It doesn't mean this is a done deal, so don't act that way. It is a huge turn off and will be used against you. Clear and confident? Yes. Pushy and grabby? No!

A client of mine knew that his work mate had a great property he could potentially rent short term while he finalised his divorce and the benefits to both parties was clear. That said he did not want to 'hard sell' to his colleague or put him under pressure because of his urgent needs. He took him for lunch to – in his words – 'run the idea past him' and after sharing his idea he simply said, 'Thanks so much for hearing me out. I'll leave it with you and if it's a good fit we can look at sorting it out.' The work mate went away to think about it and came back with a yes!

It's all about them. Our request is made to help us out and will serve us, sure. And yet don't make it all about you. Show that you have done your homework and that you acknowledge and are familiar with their situation.

A friend of mine has a podcast with millions of listens a week and PR companies are often approaching her to get their clients on the show. And yet in so many of those requests, it is clear the sender has no clue about her ethos or aim of the pod. She just deletes those emails – they don't even get a reply. The requests that show time and consideration have been spent get her attention.

Offer an exchange of sorts. One of the things that helps increase receptivity in any situation is a feeling of exchange and equity as part of a deal or energetic transaction. This does not mean you have to offer a financial reward or incentive to coax someone along. And yet you can honour the fact the other person holds power and that their use of it is to be respected.

For example, let's say you want to call in a favour and ask your mother-in-law to babysit this weekend. Instead of asking her if she is free, you could offer in return to give her a lift to see her friend the following week or even make a donation to her favourite charity.

Or simply saying, 'If there is anything I can say or do to help you in future – of course, I will!' helps a request go down well.

Ask for back up. Remember there is never only one gatekeeper. This potentially applies more in work and business when we have a person, company or department that we know can help us out. Often this is indeed the case, but their current load and priorities might mean they cannot personally assist in a timely way.

Give them an 'out' but at the same time give yourself another 'in' by simply asking, 'If you are not the right person or if this is a difficult time, who else can I go to with this, please? And I'll get out of your hair!' Most likely they will copy in another colleague and you will be off to the races, so to speak.

If there is one singular company or organisation you are really keen to connect with then another option you have is to search LinkedIn for other contacts. You can then approach them as well if the original person seems not to be available. Keep knocking on different doors and one of them will open.

Give thanks and detach. When signing off and completing your ask, whether verbal or written, finish with kindness and respect. This is where it pays to say, 'Thank you for your consideration' or,

'I'm grateful for your time' as a way to show further acknowledgement that the reader might have different things pressings them for time and resources.

We can reinforce non-attachment at this point too by closing the space of the ask. This ensures the receiver of our requests does not feel beholden to us and knows we are not clingy or desperate either. For example, 'I look forward to hearing from you when the time feels right,' or, 'I hope this has provided some food for thought. Please let me know,' rather than, 'Look forward to hearing from you very soon!' or simply and abruptly 'Thoughts?'

Always, always follow up. OK so you have made your ask and sent up your flair for 'please help me out!' but it's gone a bit quiet despite, even if you do say so yourself, your excellent delivery.

When we do not hear back from someone it is so important to have some empathy. People are busy and have deadlines and pressures they are facing that we don't have a clue about. Sometimes what you need is not going to be important enough to make it onto someone else's to-do list immediately. Sometimes as well, even though someone can help you they simply don't want to. That's a bit of a harsh one but that's their karma, not yours.

The majority of the time, your request has made it onto the 'I-must-get-round-to-that' pile in someone's brain and you can move yourself and your thing onto the 'let's-do-this' pile by simply following up. This can be the difference that makes all the difference.

Upping your asking game

Remember, people mostly want to help you out – especially those who know you! So, don't be afraid to broadcast your need when it calls for it too. Let your village rally around you and your network start working for you. If you genuinely feel at a bit of a loose end and your Google powers are just not cutting it, then don't be afraid to put it out there on social media.

'Does anyone know a good plumber in this area?'

'Do you or anyone you know have a contact at Nike?'

'Has anyone used this tech thing for their business? Is it worth the investment? I'd love your views, please!'

So much of our road to our own success is a process of joining the dots, and asking is a perfect way to proactively do your bit. You will be bowled over by what 'putting it out there' can do for you and help with where you want to take your life, free from comparison.

Let's reflect. How has your asking gone wrong in the past?

....

....

....

....

How can you tune-up your asking process and attitude?

....

....

....

....

Thinking about a current ask you have, what do you want the other person to understand from your request?

....

....

....

....

> **Thinking about a current ask you have, what do you want them to feel?**
>
> ....
>
> ....
>
> ....
>
> ....

Asking does wonders for our sense of focus and momentum as it demonstrates to yourself, and the world around you, that you are not just going to wait around for something to drop into your lap. You can take heart and sleep well knowing you did something to move forward and that is of immeasurable value and demonstrates your commitment.

No half-arsed efforts. It's time to full-arse it

We touched on this as we set out on this journey together. Your relationships with your diary and your schedule are important. Now that you have a list of your own goals, there might be a false need to urgently achieve all of the things!

I commend your attitude and energy! And yet, for maximum success, I urge you to prioritise and aim for completion on one or two things at a time and watch the successes and progress points pile up for you.

Rather than nibbling away at an array of projects, making little headway, it is better to be 'all in' on your priorities and reap the fruits of your efforts.

How this looks in your real life is perhaps having two or three goals on the go at any time and then do one thing every day that is in service of this goal.

This could be as simple as googling the microphone you might like to choose for the podcast you intend to start, clearing out your cupboards so you can make space for the partner you are calling in, spell-checking your LinkedIn profile.

Small and mighty steps completed properly will reap rewards for you. This regular connection with the progress that means the most to you will also mean you can use your weekends to rest and recuperate rather than having to binge on your efforts at the weekend.

A lasting declaration

You are now called to make a declaration to yourself and seal your promise to live entirely less 'them' and more you.

Complete the following exercise to record how you will commit to living #comparisonfree.

I am grateful for . . . I will continue . . . I will hold on to . . .	I release . . . I free myself from . . .	I call in . . . I welcome . . .

Remember . . .

'Cool' is a made-up thing.

'Popular' is a made-up thing.

'On-trend' is a made-up thing.

'In-with-the-in-crowd' is a made-up thing.

What's 'going viral' or 'really engaging' is a made-up thing.

Numbers on social media denoting value or influence
is a made-up thing.

What's the 'next big thing' on the internet is a made-up thing.

But you know what's REAL? You. Your dream. Your life visions.
Your resourcefulness. Your abilities. Your pathway. Your story.
So, do what you can to connect with that real truth today?
YOUR real truth.

In a world where comparison is making you feel like an outsider, or
the one that's behind everyone else, put two fingers on your pulse
right now and tune in to the real you and feel all that fog fall away.

Now go live your life.

Love Lucy xo
@lucysheridan

ABOUT THE AUTHOR

Lucy Sheridan is the world's first and only comparison coach who, through her private practice and workshops, has helped thousands of people go from compare and despair to #comparisonfree. Accredited by The Association for Psychological Therapies, named as one of the New Wellbeing Specialists 2018 by *ST Style* and praised as one of the UK's most successful coaches by *The Times*, her work has been featured in global outlets such as *Psychology Today*, *Forbes* and Google Labs.

ACKNOWLEDGEMENTS

'They' say it takes a village and they are right. I would love to take this opportunity to share my gratitude with the following people, without whom this would not be possible.

To Abi B – thank you for your belief and care since day one. Having you as my agent is still a thrill.

To Megan and Team Gleam for your care and time over the entire process.

To Mum, Dad, Olly, Al and Oscar – thank you for always backing me and for making me feel safe to be me. To Liz, Richard and Charlie for being the best in-laws.

To Roe – you are my heart and my healer. I love you precious, wee girl.

To Gail Love Schock, not only for your friendship but for sharing your views on the massive esoteric questions I would leave you on WhatsApp Voice note.

To my extended family and especially my Irish Grandparents. Thank you for your sacrifice, for your love and for everything it took to make the decisions that you did. To know your blood runs in my veins is a source of constant strength and support.

To my own TYG for always steering me in the direction of knowing.

To Zoe Sugg for being such a generous cheerleader who played such a big part in the tipping point that has been the last couple of years.

To Kate Bush, Stevie Nicks and Grace Jones for dissolving the writer's block and keeping me dancing, always.

Finally, to the dream team at Orion Spring especially Olivia, Emily and Ru for your guidance, energy and enthusiasm.

REFERENCES

1. No author listed, Definition of comparison in English, https://en.oxforddictionaries.com/definition/comparison (date accessed 3/01/2019)

2. David Hume, *A Treatise of Human Nature*, https://ebooks.adelaide.edu.au/h/hume/david/treatise-of-human-nature/B2.2.8.html (date accessed 3/01/2019)

3. Festinger, L. (1954). A Theory of Social Comparison Processes. *Human Relations*, 7(2), 117–140. https://doi.org/10.1177/001872675400700202

4. Kendra Cherry, Social Comparison Theory in Psychology, Verywellmind.com, https://www.verywellmind.com/what-is-the-social-comparison-process-2795872 (date accessed 14/02/2019)

5. NHS website, 'Facebook envy' associated with symptoms of depression, https://www.nhs.uk/news/mental-health/facebook-envy-associated-with-symptoms-of-depression/ (date accessed 12/07/2018)

6. UPMC WEBSITE, Social Media Use Associated With Depression Among U.S. Young Adults, https://www.upmc.com/media/news/lin-primack-sm-depression. (date accessed 12/07/2018)

7. Rheana Murray, TODAY website, Social media is affecting the way we view our bodies — and it's not good https://www.today.com/style/social-media-affecting-way-we-view-our-bodies-it-s-t128500 (date accessed 12/07/2018)

8. About page, The Narrative Enneagram, https://www.enneagram-worldwide.com/about-us/ Date accessed 1/04/2019)

9. Definition of authentic in English, https://en.oxforddictionaries.com/definition/authentic (date accessed 6/04/2019)

10. Tara Mohr, *Playing Big*, (Arrow, 2015)

11. Definition of success in English, Lexico Powered by OXFORD, https://en.oxforddictionaries.com/definition/success

12. S.M.A.R.T goals – the world's most popular way to set goals!, SMART GOALS GUIDE.COM, https://www.smart-goals-guide.com/smart-goal.html, (date accessed 18/06/19)

13. Modified from the Coaching Feedback Format, Bayer Institute for Health Care Communication, https://fhs.mcmaster.ca/facdev/documents/FeedbackGrid.pdf

14. Brad Aronson, Famous Failures: 23 Stories to Inspire You to Succeed, https://www.bradaronson.com/famous-failures/ (Date accessed 3/06/19)

15. Karen Lamb, https://www.goodreads.com/author/quotes/64270.Karen_Lamb (Date accessed 3/06/19)

16. Gay Hendricks, *The Big Leap: Conqueur Your Hidden Fear and Take Life to the Next Level*, (e-book, 2009) pp.45, 48, 52, 55

17. Interpretation built on phrase by Corinne Worsley. Used with her permission

18. Jim Rohn Quotes, https://www.goodreads.com/quotes/1798-you-are-the-average-of-the-five-people-you-spend (date accessed 19/07/2019)

19. *Acts of Faith Daily Meditations for People of Color*, Vanzant, Iyanla. Copyright 1993 https://books.google.co.uk/books?id=C-q6K6iBQ3qEC&printsec=frontcover#v=onepage&q=a%20reason&f=false p.16, p.17, p.18

20. Gary Chapman, *The Five Love Languages: How to Express Heartfelt Commitment to Your Mate* (Chicago, 2010 edition) pp.37, 55, 75, 91, 109

21. Gay Hendricks, *The Big Leap: Conquer Your Hidden Fear and Take Life to the Next Level*, (e-book, 2009) page 1

22. ibid. p.19

23. Modified from Allyn Walsh, M.D. WORKING WITH IMGS: DELIVERING EFFECTIVE FEEDBACK, April 2006, p.31, https://afmc.ca/timg/pdf/EFB_en.pdf